2008

A Book of Grace-Filled Days

LAVONNE NEFF

WITH ADVENT 2009 BY ALICE CAMILLE

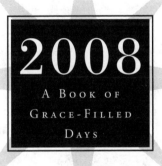

2008

A BOOK OF
GRACE-FILLED
DAYS

LOYOLAPRESS.
CHICAGO

LOYOLAPRESS.
3441 N. ASHLAND AVENUE
CHICAGO, ILLINOIS 60657
(800) 621-1008
WWW.LOYOLABOOKS.ORG

Cover and interior design by Kathy Kikkert

Library of Congress Cataloging-in-Publication Data
Neff, LaVonne.
  2008 : a book of grace-filled days / LaVonne Neff.
     p. cm.
  ISBN-13: 978-0-8294-1874-3
  ISBN-10: 0-8294-1874-1
  1. Devotional calendars—Catholic Church. 2. Catholic Church—
Prayers and devotions. 3. Bible—Meditations. 4. Catholic Church.
Lectionary for Mass (U.S.). Year A. I. Title. II. Title: Two thousand
eight. III. Title: Book of grace-filled days.
  BX2170.C56N45 2007
  242'.3—dc22

                                              2006102420

Printed in the United States of America
07 08 09 10 11 12 Bang 10 9 8 7 6 5 4 3 2 1

INTRODUCTION

I would like to dedicate this book to Dr. Helen Kenik Mainelli.

Helen—a Scripture scholar, seminary professor, librarian, and writer—did not exactly retire when she started drawing Social Security. Instead, she became the director of adult faith formation in a large and active parish in the Chicago suburbs. One of her many projects was to involve parishioners in serious, long-term study of the Bible.

To that end, she wrote weekly commentaries on the Sunday lectionary for the parish bulletin. She met with deacons and other leaders to study Scripture. And she began a series of classes based on the Denver Catholic Biblical School Program that hundreds of parishioners signed up for and kept coming back to year after year.

I have been studying the Old Testament with Helen this year, and I suspect she won't be wildly enthusiastic about this book. Helen believes—as I do—that Scripture is not meant to be dipped into a teaspoonful at a time. The Bible is not a book of pithy sayings to help us get through the day, nor is it a guide that will tell us what to do if only our eyes land on the right verse.

Scripture is a divinely inspired record of God's dealings with humanity. To benefit from it, we need to know what it says. Not just short excerpts, but the whole story; not just a few verses, but the entire book; not just a few popular books, but the whole world of Scripture with all its rich interrelationships. We also need to know something about ancient culture: history, religions, art, literature.

A tall order? Well, as they say, the journey of a thousand miles starts with a single step. I recommend starting at your local parish. Do groups meet regularly to read and discuss the Bible? If so, check them out; if not, call your diocesan office and see what resources are available.

Another way to start learning about Scripture is through reading. A good introduction, simple and short for people who don't have all day, is Steve Mueller's *The Seeker's Guide to Reading the Bible* (Loyola Press). A study Bible can be a big help. *The Catholic Bible: Personal Study Edition* (Oxford) contains not only the whole Bible but also informative guides to each book. Or you could pick up one of the teen Bibles published by Saint Mary's Press: *The Catholic Youth Bible* (high school) or *Breakthrough! The Bible for Young Catholics* (ages ten to thirteen)—fine introductions, even for parents and grandparents.

If you are already well versed in Scripture, perhaps this is the time to form a study group and encourage others to immerse themselves in God's word.

This little book, with its short readings and meditations, is no substitute for thorough, thoughtful study. Nevertheless, it can serve as a springboard into Scripture. It is based on the Catholic lectionary—the yearly selection of Bible readings for the Mass—intended to familiarize Mass-goers, over time, with major portions of Scripture.

Ideally, you will look up and read all the lectionary texts for the day (they are listed at the bottom of each page) *before* reading the daily verse(s) and meditation. Or you might choose to focus on just one of the daily passages, the one from which the text for the day is drawn. For example, the text for January 1 is Luke 2:19. The corresponding lectionary reading is Luke 2:16–21. If you read those six verses from your Bible before reading the meditation in this book, you'll have a better idea of what's going on.

For the sake of continuity, I have usually based Sunday meditations on the Gospel reading, weekday meditations on the first reading (whether Old or New Testament), and festal or seasonal meditations (such as those during Advent and Lent) on whatever text best fits the occasion. For example, every weekday from August 11 through August 23 (except August 15, Assumption) uses a passage from Ezekiel, and the meditations for twenty-eight Sundays are based on readings from Matthew.

I hope that by the end of August you will have a feel for the book of Ezekiel, and by the end of the year you will have a pretty good grasp of the Gospel according to St. Matthew. I hope that this year's readings will make you eager to learn more about 1 and 2 Samuel (nineteen selections), Isaiah (twenty-three), and Acts (forty-three). I hope you will get so interested in Scripture that you will continue to study it deeply and prayerfully.

And then I hope Helen won't mind that this book is dedicated to her.

DECEMBER 2

{O}ur salvation is nearer now than when we first believed.

—ROMANS 13:11

How many times have you come to Mass, noticed the candles and the wreaths, and thought, *Could it be Advent already?* Year by year, as we repeat the familiar rituals and read the same texts, we move steadily closer to Christ's second Advent.

Isaiah 2:1–5
Psalm 122
Romans 13:11–14
Matthew 24:37–44

I say to you, many will come from the east and the west, and will recline with Abraham, Isaac, and Jacob at the banquet in the kingdom of heaven.

—MATTHEW 8:11

St. Francis Xavier was especially interested in the East. In his forty-six years, he preached the gospel in India, the Malay Peninsula, and Japan. He hoped to preach in China also, but he died of a fever shortly after arriving there. He wrote to his good friend St. Ignatius of Loyola: "Many, many people hereabouts are not becoming Christians for one reason only: there is nobody to make them Christians."

Isaiah 4:2–6
Psalm 122
Matthew 8:5–11

{A} shoot shall sprout from the stump of Jesse,
and from his roots a bud shall blossom.

—ISAIAH 11:1

Jesse was the father of King David and an ancestor of Jesus. St. Paul reminds us how deeply our faith is rooted in Judaism: "{I}f . . . you {Christians}, a wild olive shoot, . . . have come to share in the rich root of the olive tree, do not boast against the branches. If you do boast, consider that you do not support the root; the root supports you" (Romans 11:17–18).

Isaiah 11:1–10
Psalm 72
Luke 10:21–24

Then he took the seven loaves and the fish, gave thanks, broke the loaves, and gave them to the disciples, who in turn gave them to the crowds.

—MATTHEW 15:36

Let one of those loaves represent your life. What is happening right now? Is Jesus taking you in his hands? Is he giving thanks for you? Is he breaking you? Is he giving you to the hungry world?

Isaiah 25:6–10a
Psalm 23
Matthew 15:29–37

Everyone who listens to these words of mine and acts on them will be like a wise man who built his house on rock. . . . And everyone who listens to these words of mine but does not act on them will be like a fool who built his house on sand.

—MATTHEW 7:24, 26

It's easy to listen and nod our heads. It's not all that hard to talk the talk. But the only thing that matters in the end is if we also walk the walk.

Isaiah 26:1–6
Psalm 118
Matthew 7:21, 24–27

For the tyrant will be no more
and the arrogant will have gone;
All who are alert to do evil will be cut off.

—ISAIAH 29:20

Come quickly, Lord Jesus, and make the earth safe from warmongers and terrorists!

Isaiah 29:17–24
Psalm 27
Matthew 9:27–31

*In him we were also chosen, destined in accord with the purpose of the
One who accomplishes all things according to the intention of his will,
so that we might exist for the praise of his glory.*

—EPHESIANS 1:11–12

God chose Mary to bear his Son. God chooses us also to
do his will.

Genesis 3:9–15, 20
Psalm 98
Ephesians 1:3–6, 11–12
Luke 1:26–38

Sunday

DECEMBER 9

May the God of endurance and encouragement grant you to think in harmony with one another, in keeping with Christ Jesus, that with one accord you may with one voice glorify the God and Father of our Lord Jesus Christ.

—ROMANS 15:5–6

How can we achieve such unity? By enduring people when they make us crazy, and by encouraging people when they need a boost.

Isaiah 11:1–10
Psalm 72
Romans 15:4–9
Matthew 3:1–12

DECEMBER 10

Strengthen the hands that are feeble,
make firm the knees that are weak,
Say to those whose hearts are frightened:
Be strong, fear not!
Here is your God . . .
he comes to save you.

—ISAIAH 35:3–4

Don't listen to prophets of doom. Our God is coming not to hurt us, but to save us from danger and destruction.

Isaiah 35:1–10
Psalm 85
Luke 5:17–26

DECEMBER 11

• ST. DAMASUS I, POPE •

Like a shepherd he feeds his flock;
in his arms he gathers the lambs,
Carrying them in his bosom,
and leading the ewes with care.

—ISAIAH 40:11

A lot of people who love and trust Jesus aren't so sure about his Father. Isn't God the dangerous one—the one who smites? Isaiah's beautiful image shows God's gentle, nurturing care for the most vulnerable. God the shepherd is dangerous only to predators.

Isaiah 40:1–11
Psalm 96
Matthew 18:12–14

Wednesday

DECEMBER 12

• OUR LADY OF GUADALUPE •

Many nations shall join themselves to the LORD on that day, and they shall be his people, and he will dwell among you, and you shall know that the LORD of hosts has sent me to you.

—ZECHARIAH 2:15

In 1531, the Blessed Virgin appeared to a humble farmer in Mexico. Nearly five hundred years later, at Juan Diego's canonization, Pope John Paul II said: "In accepting the Christian message without forgoing his indigenous identity, Juan Diego discovered the profound truth of the new humanity, in which all are called to be children of God."

Zechariah 2:14–17 or Revelation 11:19a; 12:1–6a, 10ab
Psalm 45
Luke 1:26–38 or 1:39–47

⇒ 11 ⇐

The afflicted and the needy seek water in vain,
their tongues are parched with thirst.
I, the LORD, will answer them;
I, the God of Israel, will not forsake them.

—ISAIAH 41:17

How does the Lord give water—and food, shelter, clothing, education, health care—to "the afflicted and the needy"? If the needy aren't getting the help they desperately need, who is responsible?

Isaiah 41:13–20
Psalm 145
Matthew 11:11–15

Friday

DECEMBER 14

• ST. JOHN OF THE CROSS, PRIEST AND DOCTOR OF THE CHURCH •

I, the LORD, your God,
*teach you what is for your good,
and lead you on the way you should go.*
—ISAIAH 48:17

This does not mean that all our days will be happy.
St. John of the Cross describes a "dark night" of interior
suffering that is a necessary part of our journey to God:
"This dark night is an inflowing of God into the soul,
which purges it from its ignorances and imperfections. . . .
Herein God secretly teaches the soul and instructs it in
perfection of love."

Isaiah 48:17–19
Psalm 1
Matthew 11:16–19

"Elijah has already come, and they did not recognize him but did to him whatever they pleased. So also will the Son of Man suffer at their hands." Then the disciples understood that he was speaking to them of John the Baptist.

—MATTHEW 17:12–13

If I had lived in Judea two thousand years ago, would I have recognized "Elijah" in John the Baptist, the fiery preacher of repentance? Would I have recognized "the Son of Man" in Jesus, the homeless healer?

Sirach 48:1–4, 9–11
Psalm 80
Matthew 17:9a, 10–13

DECEMBER 16

• THIRD SUNDAY OF ADVENT •

Do not complain, brothers, about one another, that you may not be judged. Behold, the Judge is standing before the gates.

—JAMES 5:9

Some people are so much more accomplished, better looking, or nicer than I am. Other people can't seem to do anything right. But if I complain about either kind of person, it's so I'll feel better about myself. It doesn't work, though. My self-esteem goes up only when I realize that God created each of us with a purpose, and it's not my place to judge how well anyone else is doing.

Isaiah 35:1–6a, 10
Psalm 146
James 5:7–10
Matthew 11:2–11

DECEMBER 17

The book of the genealogy of Jesus Christ . . .
—MATTHEW 1:1

Five women are listed in Jesus' genealogy. Tamar was almost executed for supposed prostitution. Rahab was indeed a prostitute. Ruth came from a nation that was one of Israel's traditional enemies. Bathsheba, "the wife of Uriah," was seduced by King David. Mary got pregnant out of wedlock. Every one of these women was socially unacceptable. Every one was an ancestor of our Lord.

Genesis 49:2, 8–10
Psalm 72
Matthew 1:1–17

{T}he days will come, says the LORD, when they shall no longer say,
"As the LORD lives, who brought the Israelites out of the land of Egypt";
but rather, "As the LORD lives, who brought the descendants of the house
of Israel up from the land of the north."

—JEREMIAH 23:7–8

It is important to remember and celebrate the ways God
has helped us and our ancestors in days gone by. It is
equally important to realize that God continues to help
us now, and that someday we will remember and celebrate
what God did for us in 2007.

Jeremiah 23:5–8
Psalm 72
Matthew 1:18–25

DECEMBER 19

And the angel said to him in reply, "I am Gabriel, who stand before God. I was sent to speak to you and to announce to you this good news. But now you will be speechless and unable to talk until the day these things take place, because you did not believe my words, which will be fulfilled at their proper time."

—LUKE 1:19–20

It was probably a good thing old Zechariah couldn't talk until his late-life baby was born. Who'd have believed him? Besides, silence allows a person to listen, and think, and maybe eventually understand—not a bad response when you get a personal message from an angel.

Judges 13:2–7, 24–25a
Psalm 71
Luke 1:5–25

DECEMBER 20

Mary said to the angel, "How can this be, since I have no relations with a man?" And the angel said to her in reply, ". . . {N}othing will be impossible for God."

—LUKE 1:34–35, 37

If we believe that God created the world and cares for each of us personally, is it all that difficult to believe in miracles?

Isaiah 7:10–14
Psalm 24
Luke 1:26–38

My lover speaks; he says to me,
"Arise, my beloved, my beautiful one,
and come!
"For see, the winter is past,
the rains are over and gone."

—SONG OF SONGS 2:10–11

Tomorrow is the shortest day of the year, and we're already looking ahead to spring! Advent is like that. In the midst of darkness, despair, and death, we look forward to our Lord's glorious return.

Song of Songs 2:8–14 or Zephaniah 3:14–18a
Psalm 33
Luke 1:39–45

The Mighty One has done great things for me,
and holy is his name.
His mercy is from age to age
to those who fear him.
—LUKE 1:49–50

"From age to age you gather a people to yourself." These words from the third Eucharistic Prayer describe what God has been doing in our world ever since creation. He calls us to him so that he can do great things for us, so that he can show us mercy.

1 Samuel 1:24–28
1 Samuel 2:1, 4–8
Luke 1:46–56

Paul, a slave of Christ Jesus, called to be an apostle and set apart for the gospel of God, . . . the gospel about his Son, descended from David according to the flesh, but established as Son of God in power according to the spirit of holiness through resurrection from the dead, Jesus Christ our Lord.

—ROMANS 1:1, 3–4

A human being who was born in Bethlehem, grew up and worked in Galilee, preached and died in Judea. The Son of God, who came back to life and lives today in heaven and on earth. In the words of an old English carol—"What child is this?"

Isaiah 7:10–14
Psalm 24
Romans 1:1–7
Matthew 1:18–24

*{S}peak thus to my servant David, ". . . Your house and your kingdom
shall endure forever before me; your throne shall stand firm forever."*
—2 SAMUEL 7:8, 16

Tonight Christians around the world celebrate the birth of
David's greatest Son.

"And he shall reign forever and ever,
King of kings, and Lord of lords!
Hallelujah!"

2 Samuel 7:1–5, 8b–12, 14a, 16
Psalm 89
Luke 1:67–79

{T}he time came for her to have her child, and she gave birth to her firstborn son. She wrapped him in swaddling clothes and laid him in a manger, because there was no room for them in the inn.

—LUKE 2:6–7

"Infant holy, infant lowly, for his bed a cattle stall;
Oxen lowing, little knowing Christ the babe is Lord of all.
Swift are winging angels singing, noels ringing, tidings
bringing:
Christ the babe is Lord of all.

"Flocks were sleeping, shepherds keeping vigil till the
morning new;
Saw the glory, heard the story, tidings of a gospel true.
Thus rejoicing, free from sorrow, praises voicing, greet the
morrow:
Christ the babe was born for you."
(Traditional Polish carol)

Vigil:
Isaiah 62:1–5
Psalm 89
Acts 13:16–17, 22–25
Matthew 1:1–25 or 1:18–25

Midnight:
Isaiah 9:1–6
Psalm 96
Titus 2:11–14
Luke 2:1–14

Dawn:
Isaiah 62:11–12
Psalm 97
Titus 3:4–7
Luke 2:15–20

Day:
Isaiah 52:7–10
Psalm 98
Hebrews 1:1–6
John 1:1–18 or 1:1–5, 9–14

DECEMBER 26

• ST. STEPHEN, FIRST MARTYR •

Into your hands I commend my spirit;
you will redeem me, LORD, faithful God.
—PSALM 31:6

Jesus said words from this psalm as he hung on the cross. St. Stephen said them as he was being stoned to death. Instead of desperately clutching their lives, they handed their spirits over to God, trusting that God would bring good out of evil, abundance out of apparent waste.

Acts 6:8–10; 7:54–59
Psalm 31
Matthew 10:17–22

DECEMBER 27

Light dawns for the just;
gladness, for the honest of heart.

—PSALM 97:11

It's hard to believe, but the days are starting to get longer.
The "light of the world" has been born into the darkness.
Quietly but surely, the earth is being transformed.

1 John 1:1–4
Psalm 97
John 20:1a, 2–8

A voice was heard in Ramah,
sobbing and loud lamentation;
Rachel weeping for her children,
and she would not be consoled,
since they were no more.

—MATTHEW 2:18

All the baby boys in Bethlehem were slaughtered, sacrifices to King Herod's insatiable lust for power. Only Jesus survived the massacre. Some thirty years later, Jesus would die a willing sacrifice so that death itself could be destroyed.

1 John 1:5–2:2
Psalm 124
Matthew 2:13–18

Whoever hates his brother is in darkness; he walks in darkness and does not know where he is going because the darkness has blinded his eyes.

—1 JOHN 2:11

The men who assassinated Thomas Becket knew Henry II was furious with him and thought they were doing the king a favor. According to a twelfth-century biographer, however, Henry was shocked when he learned of Becket's death: he "burst into loud lamentations, and exchanged his royal robes for sackcloth and ashes. . . . Three whole days he spent in his chamber, and would receive neither food nor consolation." The king had not considered where his anger might lead.

1 John 2:3–11
Psalm 96
Luke 2:22–35

DECEMBER 30

• THE HOLY FAMILY OF JESUS, MARY, AND JOSEPH •

Like a fruitful vine
your wife within your home,
Like olive plants
your children around your table.
Just so will they be blessed
who fear the LORD.
—PSALM 128:3–4

"Walls for the wind,
A roof for the rain,
And drinks beside the fire;
Laughter to cheer you,
Those you love near you,
And all that your heart may desire."
(Traditional Irish blessing)

Sirach 3:2–7, 12–14
Psalm 128
Colossians 3:12–21 or 3:12–17
Matthew 2:13–15, 19–23

In the beginning was the Word,
and the Word was with God,
and the Word was God.

—JOHN 1:1

The year 2007 has almost ended. Tonight many of us
will gather with friends, stay up late, drink champagne,
sing "Auld Lang Syne," and joke about last year's unkept
resolutions. Whether the year has been painful or joyful,
we're eager to move on, ready to begin again.

1 John 2:18–21
Psalm 96
John 1:1–18

JANUARY 1

And Mary kept all these things, reflecting on them in her heart.
—LUKE 2:19

Years would pass before Mary understood the remarkable events surrounding Jesus' birth. But just as she had kept Jesus safe in her womb, she kept her memories safe in her heart. When we do not understand our experiences, we can wait and trust God to reveal whatever we need to know—when we need to know it.

Numbers 6:22–27
Psalm 67
Galatians 4:4–7
Luke 2:16–21

JANUARY 2

Let what you heard from the beginning remain in you. If what you heard from the beginning remains in you, then you will remain in the Son and in the Father.

—1 JOHN 2:24

It's true that a journey of a thousand miles begins with a single step—but then we have to keep walking.

1 John 2:22–28
Psalm 98
John 1:19–28

Beloved, we are God's children now; what we shall be has not yet been revealed. We do know that when it is revealed we shall be like him, for we shall see him as he is.

—1 JOHN 3:2

Here is a mystery: "The Son of God became man, that we might become God" (St. Athanasius of Alexandria).

1 John 2:29–3:6
Psalm 98
John 1:29–34

In this way, the children of God and the children of the devil are made plain; no one who fails to act in righteousness belongs to God, nor anyone who does not love his brother.

—1 JOHN 3:10

How can we know that we are God's children? Two ways: by our ethical behavior and by our love for God's other children.

1 John 3:7–10
Psalm 98
John 1:35–42

*If someone who has worldly means sees a brother in need and refuses him
compassion, how can the love of God remain in him?*

—1 JOHN 3:17

Not even Bill Gates can help everybody in need. But even I
can help somebody.

1 John 3:11–21
Psalm 100
John 1:43–51

JANUARY 6

• THE EPIPHANY OF THE LORD •

See, darkness covers the earth,
and thick clouds cover the peoples;
But upon you the LORD shines,
and over you appears his glory.
Nations shall walk by your light,
and kings by your shining radiance.

—ISAIAH 60:2-3

When the church walks in the light of Christ, every dark
corner of the earth is illuminated.

Isaiah 60:1–6
Psalm 72
Ephesians 3:2–3a, 5–6
Matthew 2:1–12

Beloved, do not trust every spirit but test the spirits to see whether they belong to God, because many false prophets have gone out into the world. This is how you can know the Spirit of God: every spirit that acknowledges Jesus Christ come in the flesh belongs to God.

—1 JOHN 4:1–2

Some people think the body is unimportant and the spirit is all that really matters. That is not a Christian way to think. Jesus was a flesh-and-blood human being. His body and blood are vital to our salvation.

1 John 3:22–4:6
Psalm 2
Matthew 4:12–17, 23–25

JANUARY 8

In this is love: not that we have loved God, but that he loved us and sent his Son as expiation for our sins.

—1 JOHN 4:10

"The source of our love for God can only be found in the fact that God loved us first. He has given us himself as the object of our love, and he has also given us its source. . . . This love is not something we generate ourselves. It comes to us through the Holy Spirit who has been given to us" (St. Augustine).

1 John 4:7–10
Psalm 72
Mark 6:34–44

JANUARY 9

No one has ever seen God. Yet, if we love one another, God remains in us, and his love is brought to perfection in us.

—1 JOHN 4:12

The world sees God by looking at us, God's people. When we love one another—and show our love by caring for those who are weak, suffering, or otherwise needy—God's love becomes visible through us.

1 John 4:11–18
Psalm 72
Mark 6:45–52

If anyone says, "I love God," but hates his brother, he is a liar; for whoever does not love a brother whom he has seen cannot love God whom he has not seen.

—1 JOHN 4:20

Sometimes it seems easier to love God than to love the people God created. For that matter, it can be easier to love people in the abstract than to love the actual people we live and work with. As Linus famously observed in a *Peanuts* cartoon, "I love mankind—it's people I can't stand."

1 John 4:19–5:4
Psalm 72
Luke 4:14–22a

God gave us eternal life, and this life is in his Son. Whoever possesses the Son has life; whoever does not possess the Son of God does not have life.

—1 JOHN 5:11–12

Jesus, the Son of God, is our only source of eternal life. To have that life, we need more than an intellectual belief in Jesus. We need to "possess" him—to have an ongoing, life-giving relationship with him.

1 John 5:5–13
Psalm 147
Luke 5:12–16

JANUARY 12

And we have this confidence in him, that if we ask anything according to his will, he hears us. And if we know that he hears us in regard to whatever we ask, we know that what we have asked him for is ours.

—1 JOHN 5:14–15

What does it mean to ask according to God's will? Would you want God to give you anything that is not according to his will?

1 John 5:14–21
Psalm 149
John 3:22–30

JANUARY 13

After Jesus was baptized, he came up from the water and behold, the heavens were opened [for him], and he saw the Spirit of God descending like a dove [and] coming upon him. And a voice came from the heavens, saying, "This is my beloved Son, with whom I am well pleased."

—MATTHEW 3:16–17

Jesus is about thirty years old. He has spent his life so far doing manual labor in a small town. Now he is ready to begin his public ministry. Does he know he will heal the sick? Feed the multitudes? Preach unforgettable sermons? Does he know he will be tortured and killed? What does the voice from the heavens mean to him?

Isaiah 42:1–4, 6–7
Psalm 29
Acts 10:34–38
Matthew 3:13–17

JANUARY 14

When the day came for Elkanah to offer sacrifice, he used to give a portion each to his wife Peninnah and to all her sons and daughters, but a double portion to Hannah because he loved her, though the LORD had made her barren.

—1 SAMUEL 1:4–5

This verse is from the beginning of a lovely story about answered prayer and the birth of a much-wanted child. In many ways, it is a story about God's grace. A wife's function, in Hannah's day, was to bear children—and she could not. But Elkanah loved her just the same. His gifts, like God's, were based on his love, not on her productivity.

1 Samuel 1:1–8
Psalm 116
Mark 1:14–20

The bows of the mighty are broken,
while the tottering gird on strength.
The well-fed hire themselves out for bread,
while the hungry batten on spoil.

—1 SAMUEL 2:4–5

Hannah responds to her son's miraculous birth much as Mary will respond to her own miraculous pregnancy—"He has thrown down the rulers from their thrones / but lifted up the lowly. / The hungry he has filled with good things; / the rich he has sent away empty" (Luke 1:52–53). Both women praise God for overturning the natural order, for bringing power to the weak and food to the hungry.

1 Samuel 1:9–20
1 Samuel 2:1, 4–8
Mark 1:21–28

The LORD called Samuel again, for the third time. Getting up and going to Eli, he said, "Here I am. You called me." Then Eli understood that the LORD was calling the youth. So he said to Samuel, "Go to sleep, and if you are called, reply, 'Speak, LORD, for your servant is listening.'"

—1 SAMUEL 3:8–9

How does a person discern a vocation? Select a career? Choose a spouse? Make any kind of important decision? Often we don't recognize God's call until a wise friend helps us listen.

1 Samuel 3:1–10, 19–20
Psalm 40
Mark 1:29–39

When the troops retired to the camp, the elders of Israel said, "Why has the LORD permitted us to be defeated today by the Philistines? Let us fetch the ark of the LORD from Shiloh that it may go into battle among us and save us from the grasp of our enemies." . . .

The Philistines fought and Israel was defeated. . . . It was a disastrous defeat, in which Israel lost thirty thousand foot soldiers. The ark of God was captured.

—1 SAMUEL 4:3, 10–11

How often, instead of obeying God, do I try to use God as my servant?

1 Samuel 4:1–11
Psalm 44
Mark 1:40–45

The people, however, refused to listen to Samuel's warning and said,
"Not so! There must be a king over us. We too must be like other
nations, with a king to rule us and to lead us in warfare and fight our
battles." When Samuel had listened to all the people had to say, he
repeated it to the LORD, who then said to him, "Grant their request and
appoint a king to rule them."

—1 SAMUEL 8:19–22

The people had a point in requesting a king to lead
them—their evil rulers, Samuel's sons, did not provide
justice or protection. But Samuel had a point too: kings
can cause more problems than they solve. As Lord Acton
noted, "Power tends to corrupt. . . . Great men are almost
always bad men." And yet God continues to work through
human leaders, however flawed they may be.

1 Samuel 8:4–7, 10–22a
Psalm 89
Mark 2:1–12

There was no other Israelite handsomer than Saul; he stood head and shoulders above the people. . . .

When Samuel caught sight of Saul, the LORD assured him, "This is the man of whom I told you; he is to govern my people."

—1 SAMUEL 9:2, 17

Alas, the handsome Saul turned away from God. The next time Samuel went in search of a king, the Lord gave him quite different criteria: "Do not judge him from his appearance or from his lofty stature. . . . Not as man sees does God see, because man sees the appearance but the LORD looks into the heart" (1 Samuel 16:7). Something to remember as the image makers get ready for this year's presidential race.

1 Samuel 9:1–4, 17–19; 10:1a
Psalm 21
Mark 2:13–17

The next day he saw Jesus coming toward him and said, "Behold, the Lamb of God, who takes away the sin of the world."

—JOHN 1:29

The night before the Israelites escaped from Egypt, each family sacrificed a lamb to save the family's firstborn from death (Exodus 12:1–13). The book of Isaiah describes a "lamb led to the slaughter" who "gives his life as an offering for sin" (53:7, 10). John called Jesus a lamb not because he was gentle but because he would die for others.

Isaiah 49:3, 5–6
Psalm 40
1 Corinthians 1:1–3
John 1:29–34

Does the LORD so delight in holocausts and sacrifices
as in obedience to the command of the LORD?
Obedience is better than sacrifice,
and submission than the fat of rams.

—1 SAMUEL 15:22

Against Samuel's explicit instructions, Saul had just collected a lot of loot—and now he hoped to buy off God. "The men spared the best sheep and oxen to sacrifice to the LORD," Saul explained (15:15). As I write, powerful politicians are rushing to donate bribe money to charity. But God, unlike some public servants, can't be bought.

1 Samuel 15:16–23
Psalm 50
Mark 2:18–22

Then Samuel asked Jesse, "Are these all the sons you have?" Jesse replied, "There is still the youngest, who is tending the sheep." Samuel said to Jesse, "Send for him; we will not begin the sacrificial banquet until he arrives here."

—1 SAMUEL 16:11

Samuel was searching for the next king of Israel, and God told him to reject seven of Jesse's sons. One son remained, and he would not have been on anyone's short list. He was still an adolescent. He spent his days herding sheep. But God, who is always turning human expectations upside down, chose David to be king and ancestor of our Lord.

1 Samuel 16:1–13
Psalm 89
Mark 2:23–28

JANUARY 23

All this multitude, too, shall learn that it is not by sword or spear that the LORD saves. For the battle is the LORD's, and he shall deliver you into our hands.

—1 SAMUEL 17:47

For David to challenge Goliath made as much sense as a lamb taking on a bear. But the point of the story is not that David was exceptionally brave or strong or clever. It is that Israel's success depended entirely on God.

1 Samuel 17:32–33, 37, 40–51
Psalm 144
Mark 3:1–6

The women played and sang:

*"Saul has slain his thousands,
and David his ten thousands."*

Saul was very angry and resentful of the song.
—1 SAMUEL 18:7–8

Saul could have had a brilliant young general working
for him. David could have increased Saul's effectiveness
tenfold. But Saul was jealous, because David was young,
handsome, and single. The groupies were following David
now, not Saul. So rather than enlisting David on his side,
Saul had a midlife meltdown.

1 Samuel 18:6–9; 19:1–7
Psalm 56
Mark 3:7–12

The Lord said to him, "Get up and go to the street called Straight and ask at the house of Judas for a man from Tarsus named Saul. . . ." But Ananias replied, "Lord, I have heard from many sources about this man, what evil things he has done to your holy ones in Jerusalem."

—ACTS 9:11, 13

How would you feel if you were told to go to a known terrorist, lay hands on him, and pray for his healing? How would you feel if someone brought that terrorist to church to be baptized? Or if the ex-terrorist held a preaching mission in your parish?

Acts 22:3–16 or 9:1–22
Psalm 117
Mark 16:15–18

I recall your sincere faith that first lived in your grandmother Lois and in your mother Eunice and that I am confident lives also in you.

—2 TIMOTHY 1:5

Whatever else Lois passed on to Eunice, and Eunice to Timothy—wavy hair, a house, a trust fund—has long since disappeared. The Christian faith, however, is an inheritance that can last forever.

2 Timothy 1:1–8 or Titus 1:1–5
Psalm 80
Mark 3:20–21

From that time on, Jesus began to preach and say, "Repent, for the kingdom of heaven is at hand."

—MATTHEW 4:17

In the New Testament, the word *repent* means to change one's mind, to turn from one way of life to another. As Christians, we are alive and growing. Walking with Jesus, we continually see aspects of our lives that need transforming. Jesus asks us to repent—to change our minds, hearts, and actions—over and over again.

Isaiah 8:23–9:3
Psalm 27
1 Corinthians 1:10–13, 17
Matthew 4:12–23 or 4:12–17

David was thirty years old when he became king.
—2 SAMUEL 5:4

"When Jesus began his ministry he was about thirty years of age" (Luke 3:23). David was just a boy when he killed Goliath, and Jesus was just a boy when he amazed the temple scholars with his knowledge (Luke 2:41–51). Both boys waited many years before taking up their lifework. When God calls us to a task, he may not mean for us to start right away. He may want us first to take time to prepare.

2 Samuel 5:1–7, 10
Psalm 89
Mark 3:22–30

JANUARY 29

Then David, girt with a linen apron, came dancing before the LORD with abandon, as he and all the Israelites were bringing up the ark of the LORD with shouts of joy and to the sound of the horn.

—2 SAMUEL 6:14–15

The ark was where God made his presence known, and it was as important to Israel as the Eucharist is to Catholics. When Eli, Samuel's mentor, learned that the Philistines had captured the ark, he fell off his chair and died (1 Samuel 4:12–18). Now the ark was entering Jerusalem, where it would be safe for centuries to come. No wonder David danced!

2 Samuel 6:12b–15, 17–19
Psalm 24
Mark 3:31–35

JANUARY 30

The LORD of hosts has this to say: It was I who took you from the pasture and from the care of the flock to be commander of my people Israel. . . . And when your time comes and you rest with your ancestors, I will raise up your heir after you. . . . And I will make his royal throne firm forever.

—2 SAMUEL 7:8, 12–13

God chose David, the last-born shepherd boy, to be Israel's greatest king. Jesus, Son of God and also son of a poor family in a remote village, is "Lord of lords and king of kings" (Revelation 17:14). God's kingdom is coming and God's will is being done, but rarely in the way we expect.

2 Samuel 7:4–17
Psalm 89
Mark 4:1–20

Then King David went in and sat before the LORD and said, "Who am I, Lord GOD, and who are the members of my house, that you have brought me to this point?"

—2 SAMUEL 7:18

Taking credit for one's successes but denying responsibility for one's failures is a pronounced human tendency. By contrast, David gave God credit for his rise to power, and he took personal responsibility for his sins (see, for example, 2 Samuel 12:13–16).

2 Samuel 7:18–19, 24–29
Psalm 132
Mark 4:21–25

The next morning David wrote a letter to Joab which he sent by Uriah.
In it he directed: "Place Uriah up front, where the fighting is fierce.
Then pull back and leave him to be struck down dead."

—2 SAMUEL 11:14–15

David, as commander in chief, had the right to send his
soldiers wherever he wished. But in this case, he was
committing cold-blooded murder. Just because something
is legal does not mean it is moral.

2 Samuel 11:1–4a, 5–10a, 13–17
Psalm 51
Mark 4:26–34

Now, Master, you may let your servant go
in peace, according to your word,
for my eyes have seen your salvation.

—LUKE 2:29–30

Simeon was ready to die once he saw "the Messiah of the Lord" (2:26). A friend of mine had a near-death experience, during which she felt God's peace so profoundly that she lost all fear of death. Our attitude toward death changes when we deeply believe that we, and the world, are safe in God's loving hands.

Malachi 3:1–4
Psalm 24
Hebrews 2:14–18
Luke 2:22–40 or 2:22–32

Blessed are the merciful,
for they will be shown mercy.

—MATTHEW 5:7

"It is not the same thing, man's mercy, and God's; but as
wide as is the interval between wickedness and goodness,
so far is the one of these removed from the other"
(St. John Chrysostom).

Zephaniah 2:3; 3:12–13
Psalm 146
1 Corinthians 1:26–31
Matthew 5:1–12a

FEBRUARY 4

Abishai, son of Zeruiah, said to the king: "Why should this dead dog curse my lord the king? Let me go over, please, and lop off his head." But the king replied: "What business is it of mine or of yours . . . that he curses?" . . . "Let him alone and let him curse, for the LORD has told him to."

—2 SAMUEL 16:9–11

David had no right to behead Shimei, but according to the law of "eye for eye" (Leviticus 24:20), David could have justifiably cursed Shimei in return. David, however, responded as Jesus would later instruct: "Offer no resistance to one who is evil" (Matthew 5:39). David's and Jesus' approach stops the cycle of evil.

2 Samuel 15:13–14, 30; 16:5–13
Psalm 3
Mark 5:1–20

FEBRUARY 5

• ST. AGATHA, VIRGIN AND MARTYR •

The king was shaken, and went up to the room over the city gate
to weep. He said as he wept, "My son Absalom! My son, my son
Absalom! If only I had died instead of you, Absalom, my son, my son!"
—2 SAMUEL 19:1

The greatly beloved Absalom died while trying to oust
King David, his father, and take over the kingdom. David's
response was not anger, but self-sacrificing love. Centuries
later, St. Paul would write: "God proves his love for us in
that while we were still sinners Christ died for us" (Romans
5:8). No wonder the prophet Samuel called David "a man
after [God's] own heart" (1 Samuel 13:14).

2 Samuel 18:9–10, 14b, 24–25a, 30–19:3
Psalm 86
Mark 5:21–43

FEBRUARY 6

• ASH WEDNESDAY •

Yet even now, says the LORD,
return to me with your whole heart,
with fasting, and weeping, and mourning;
Rend your hearts, not your garments,
and return to the LORD, *your God.*
For gracious and merciful is he,
slow to anger, rich in kindness,
and relenting in punishment.

—JOEL 2:12–13

This is a day for mourning our sin and contemplating our death. But it is also a day for giving thanks to Jesus Christ, who rescued us from sin and death.

Joel 2:12–18
Psalm 51
2 Corinthians 5:20–6:2
Matthew 6:1–6, 16–18

I have set before you life and death, the blessing and the curse. Choose life, then, that you and your descendants may live, by loving the LORD, your God, heeding his voice, and holding fast to him.

—DEUTERONOMY 30:19–20

"Life" and "choice" are not opposites. Life is a choice, and often a difficult one. Choosing life requires love, obedience, and perseverance.

Deuteronomy 30:15–20
Psalm 1
Luke 9:22–25

• ST. JEROME EMILIANI, PRIEST • ST. JOSEPHINE BAKHITA, VIRGIN •

"Why do we fast, and you do not see it?
afflict ourselves, and you take no note of it?"

Lo, on your fast day you carry out your own pursuits,
and drive all your laborers.

—ISAIAH 58:3

What is the point of fast days if we think only of ourselves
when we fast? How can fasting help us become less selfish?

Isaiah 58:1–9a
Psalm 51
Matthew 9:14–15

If you hold back your foot on the sabbath
from following your own pursuits on my holy day;
If you call the sabbath a delight,
and the LORD's holy day honorable;
If you honor it by not following your ways,
seeking your own interests, or speaking with malice—
Then you shall delight in the LORD,
and I will make you ride on the heights of the earth.

—ISAIAH 58:13–14

Rather than observing a weekly Sabbath, many of us work 24/7. By focusing so intently on our own work, do we lose sight of the fact that every blessing comes from God?

Isaiah 58:9b–14
Psalm 86
Luke 5:27–32

FEBRUARY 10

• FIRST SUNDAY OF LENT •

Then Jesus was led by the Spirit into the desert to be tempted by the devil. . . . The tempter approached and said to him, "If you are the Son of God, command that these stones become loaves of bread."

—MATTHEW 4:1, 3

Forty days earlier, Jesus had heard a voice from the heavens saying, "This is my beloved Son, with whom I am well pleased" (Matthew 3:17). Now, weakened from his long fast, he heard the tempter's cynical voice: "If you are the Son of God . . ." Did he have a moment of doubt? Did he want to take up the tempter's challenge? What gave him the power to resist?

Genesis 2:7–9; 3:1–7
Psalm 51
Romans 5:12–19 or 5:12, 17–19
Matthew 4:1–11

FEBRUARY 11

• OUR LADY OF LOURDES •

The LORD said to Moses, "Speak to the whole Israelite community and
tell them: Be holy, for I, the LORD, your God, am holy."

—LEVITICUS 19:1–2

We hardly ever use the word *holy* except in the expression
"holier than thou." What did the Lord mean?
The rest of the passage helps us understand: a holy person
is one who treats other people with respect and justice.
To sum it up: "You shall love your neighbor as yourself.
I am the LORD" (19:18).

Leviticus 19:1–2, 11–18
Psalm 19
Matthew 25:31–46

FEBRUARY 12

For just as from the heavens
the rain and snow come down
And do not return there
till they have watered the earth,
making it fertile and fruitful, . . .
So shall my word be
that goes forth from my mouth;
It shall not return to me void,
but shall do my will,
achieving the end for which I sent it.
—ISAIAH 55:10–11

God's word is life-giving. God's promises will be fulfilled.

Isaiah 55:10–11
Psalm 34
Matthew 6:7–15

FEBRUARY 13

When God saw by their actions how they turned from their evil way, he repented of the evil that he had threatened to do to them; he did not carry it out.

—JONAH 3:10

Unlike Jonah, who was powerfully embarrassed when his prophecy of doom did not come true, God is always delighted to "repent"—to change his plan of action in response to human repentance. Jesus said that there is "more joy in heaven over one sinner who repents than over ninety-nine righteous people who have no need of repentance" (Luke 15:7).

Jonah 3:1–10
Psalm 51
Luke 11:29–32

*Then she prayed to the LORD, the God of Israel, saying: "My LORD,
our King, you alone are God. Help me, who am alone and have no help
but you."*

—ESTHER C:14

Sometimes God gives us what we ask for—safety, rescue,
health, material things. But sometimes he seems to not
even hear our pleas. Do we then turn from him, figuring
he isn't interested in our needs? Or do we hang on to him
more tightly, believing that God alone can provide us with
the strength to deal with anything life throws our way?

Esther C:12, 14–16, 23–25
Psalm 138
Matthew 7:7–12

Friday

FEBRUARY 15

Do I indeed derive any pleasure from the death of the wicked? says the Lord GOD. Do I not rather rejoice when he turns from his evil way that he may live?

—EZEKIEL 18:23

How do you suppose God feels when a murderer is executed or a tyrant is assassinated or an attacker is killed in battle?

Ezekiel 18:21–28
Psalm 130
Matthew 5:20–26

*Today you are making this agreement with the LORD: he is to be your
God and you are to walk in his ways and . . . hearken to his voice.
And today the LORD is making this agreement with you: you are
to be a people peculiarly his own, . . . and provided you keep all his
commandments, he will then raise you high in praise and
renown and glory.*

—DEUTERONOMY 26:17–19

Do we keep God's commandments so he will reward us?
Or do we keep them because we are his people and he is
our God? What's the difference?

Deuteronomy 26:16–19
Psalm 119
Matthew 5:43–48

FEBRUARY 17

• SECOND SUNDAY OF LENT •

While he was still speaking, behold, a bright cloud cast a shadow over them, then from the cloud came a voice that said, "This is my beloved Son, with whom I am well pleased; listen to him."

—MATTHEW 17:5

Jesus heard those same words from heaven after his baptism. Then, in the wilderness, the tempter insinuated that Jesus was not the Son of God. Now, on the mountaintop, he hears God's loving words again. Soon he will be hanging on a cross, wondering why God has forsaken him. If your spiritual life has extreme ups and downs, know that you are not alone.

Genesis 12:1–4a
Psalm 33
2 Timothy 1:8b–10
Matthew 17:1–9

O LORD, we are shamefaced, like our kings, our princes, and our fathers, for having sinned against you. But yours, O Lord, our God, are compassion and forgiveness!

—DANIEL 9:8–9

How many American leaders have ever admitted error, let alone sin? How often have we looked for excuses so we would not have to admit our mistakes? And yet how do we receive God's compassion and forgiveness if we don't recognize our sin?

Daniel 9:4b–10
Psalm 79
Luke 6:36–38

Hear the word of the LORD,
princes of Sodom!
Listen to the instruction of our God,
people of Gomorrah! . . .

Put away your misdeeds from before my eyes;
cease doing evil; learn to do good.
Make justice your aim: redress the wronged,
hear the orphan's plea, defend the widow.
—ISAIAH 1:10, 16–17

The prophet is not advising good people to make a few
cosmetic improvements. He is calling on legendary
sinners—people like those in Sodom and Gomorrah—to
give their lives a complete makeover.

Isaiah 1:10, 16–20
Psalm 50
Matthew 23:1–12

"Come," they said, "let us contrive a plot against Jeremiah. . . .{L}et us destroy him by his own tongue; let us carefully note his every word."

—JEREMIAH 18:18

Jeremiah was a whistle-blower. His God-appointed task was to speak truth to the powerful. If the rulers had listened to him, they could have saved their nation from disaster. But instead of heeding his message and repenting, they tried to kill the messenger.

Jeremiah 18:18–20
Psalm 31
Matthew 20:17–28

More tortuous than all else is the human heart,
beyond remedy; who can understand it?
I, the LORD, alone probe the mind
and test the heart,
To reward everyone according to his ways,
according to the merit of his deeds.

—JEREMIAH 17:9–10

Tortuous means complicated, winding, twisting, even devious. When we say, "God only knows why I did that," we are absolutely correct. If we can't understand our own motivations, how do we dare judge others?

Jeremiah 17:5–10
Psalm 1
Luke 16:19–31

So I exhort the presbyters among you. . . . Tend the flock of God in your midst, [overseeing] not by constraint but willingly, as God would have it, not for shameful profit but eagerly. Do not lord it over those assigned to you, but be examples to the flock.

—1 PETER 5:1–3

Excellent advice from St. Peter, not only for ordained clergy, but also for all other Christians who might possibly have an influence on someone else—including you and me.

1 Peter 5:1–4
Psalm 23
Matthew 16:13–19

*Who is there like you, the God who removes guilt
and pardons sin for the remnant of his inheritance;
Who does not persist in anger forever,
but delights rather in clemency,
And will again have compassion on us,
treading underfoot our guilt?
You will cast into the depths of the sea
all our sins.*

—MICAH 7:18–19

Lent is a time to recognize our sins, not to focus on guilt.
Lent points us to Easter, to God's amazing grace and
forgiveness.

Micah 7:14–15, 18–20
Psalm 103
Luke 15:1–3, 11–32

Jesus answered and said to her, "Everyone who drinks this water will be thirsty again; but whoever drinks the water I shall give will never thirst; the water I shall give will become in him a spring of water welling up to eternal life."

—JOHN 4:13–14

A friend who was hospitalized with a serious illness was terrified. "I'll pray for healing," her pastor offered. "Do," she said. "But please pray also that I will feel God's peace. If I'm healed, I'll get sick again, maybe many times, and each time I'll panic—unless I learn to put myself in God's hands."

Exodus 17:3–7
Psalm 95
Romans 5:1–2, 5–8
John 4:5–42 or 4:5–15, 19b–26, 39a, 40–42

The prophet sent him the message: "Go and wash seven times in the Jordan, and your flesh will heal, and you will be clean." But Naaman went away angry, saying, "I thought that he would surely come out and stand there to invoke the LORD his God, and would move his hand over the spot, and thus cure the leprosy."

—2 KINGS 5:10–11

Naaman knew what he wanted God to do for him, and he knew exactly how he wanted God to do it. He was so sure that he, not God, should be in charge that he almost gave up the blessing God wanted to give him.

2 Kings 5:1–15b
Psalm 42
Luke 4:24–30

FEBRUARY 26

But with contrite heart and humble spirit
let us be received; . . .
for those who trust in you cannot be put to shame.

—DANIEL 3:39–40

Azariah (also known as Abednego), with his two
companions, Shadrach and Meshach, had just been thrown
into a white-hot furnace for refusing to worship the god of
the Babylonian king. Escape was humanly impossible, but
God heard their prayers and delivered them.

Daniel 3:25, 34–43
Psalm 25
Matthew 18:21–35

Therefore, I teach you the statutes and decrees as the LORD, my God, has commanded me. . . . Observe them carefully, for thus will you give evidence of your wisdom and intelligence to the nations, who will hear of all these statutes and say, "This great nation is truly a wise and intelligent people."

—DEUTERONOMY 4:5–6

Public opinion is important—that's why we have so many spin doctors. What would happen if a nation or a church or an individual worried less about maintaining one's image and more about doing what is right?

Deuteronomy 4:1, 5–9
Psalm 147
Matthew 5:17–19

FEBRUARY 28

From the day that your fathers left the land of Egypt even to this day, I have sent you untiringly all my servants the prophets. Yet they have not obeyed me nor paid heed; they have stiffened their necks and done worse than their fathers. When you speak all these words to them, they will not listen to you either.

—JEREMIAH 7:25–27

Why do you suppose we observe Lent year after year after year?

Jeremiah 7:23–28
Psalm 95
Luke 11:14–23

FEBRUARY 29

Return, O Israel, to the LORD, your God. . . .

I will heal their defection,
I will love them freely;
for my wrath is turned away from them.
—HOSEA 14:2, 5

"When true simplicity is gained,
To bow and to bend we shan't be ashamed,
To turn, turn will be our delight,
Till by turning, turning we come round right."
("Simple Gifts")

Hosea 14:2–10
Psalm 81
Mark 12:28–34

Let us know, let us strive to know the LORD;
as certain as the dawn is his coming,
and his judgment shines forth like the light of day!
He will come to us like the rain,
like spring rain that waters the earth.

—HOSEA 6:3

Hosea pictures judgment not as a fearful time of punishment but as a time of light, refreshment, and new growth for those who know the Lord.

Hosea 6:1–6
Psalm 51
Luke 18:9–14

One thing I do know is that I was blind and now I see.
—JOHN 9:25

"Was blind and now I see"—John Newton used these words in what has become America's favorite hymn, "Amazing Grace." Newton was an irreligious slave trader who cried out to God during a violent storm at sea. His ship was saved, and so was he. Right away he began treating his slaves humanely. Then he gave up slave trading altogether. Eventually he became a priest.

1 Samuel 16:1b, 6–7, 10–13a
Psalm 23
Ephesians 5:8–14
John 9:1–41 or 9:1, 6–9, 13–17, 34–38

*Lo, I am about to create new heavens
and a new earth;
The things of the past shall not be remembered
or come to mind.*

—ISAIAH 65:17

In the book of Revelation, John uses similar words to describe his vision of the future re-creation of the world: "Then I saw a new heaven and a new earth. The former heaven and the former earth had passed away" (21:1). In this new earth, "there shall be no more death or mourning, wailing or pain, [for] the old order has passed away" (21:4).

Isaiah 65:17–21
Psalm 30
John 4:43–54

Tuesday

MARCH 4

• ST. CASIMIR •

Wherever the river flows, every sort of living creature that can multiply shall live, and there shall be abundant fish, for wherever this water comes the sea shall be made fresh.

—EZEKIEL 47:9

In Ezekiel's vision, water flowed out of the temple, making the earth fertile. Jesus offered "living water" to the woman at the well: "{W}hoever drinks the water I shall give will never thirst; the water I shall give will become in him a spring of water welling up to eternal life" (John 4:14). Faith, like flowing water, is creative and life-giving.

Ezekiel 47:1–9, 12
Psalm 46
John 5:1–16

I will cut a road through all my mountains,
and make my highways level.

—ISAIAH 49:11

Do you sometimes feel that there are enormous obstacles
between you and God? No mountain is too high for God
to cut through.

Isaiah 49:8–15
Psalm 145
John 5:17–30

*They have soon turned aside from the way I pointed out to them,
making for themselves a molten calf and worshiping it, sacrificing to it
and crying out, "This is your God, O Israel, who brought you out of
the land of Egypt!"*

—EXODUS 32:8

Only a short time before, God had proclaimed to Israel:
"I, the LORD, am your God, who brought you out of the
land of Egypt" (Exodus 20:2). But then Moses, the people's
leader and God's prophet, disappeared, and the people
wanted something visible to believe in, something concrete
they could make for themselves. The calf idol seemed real,
while the invisible God did not.

Exodus 32:7–14
Psalm 106
John 5:31–47

With revilement and torture let us put him to the test
that we may have proof of his gentleness
and try his patience.
—WISDOM 2:19

These are the thoughts of the wicked, but they could also be those of the wounded. Often a deeply hurt person—or animal—does not know how to respond to gentleness. Is it real? Will it last? Or will this apparently kind person turn on me and injure me later? The only way to know is to test the limits, over and over again.

Wisdom 2:1a, 12–22
Psalm 34
John 7:1–2, 10, 25–30

Grant me justice, LORD, for I am blameless,
free of any guilt.
—PSALM 7:9

Now that is a dangerous prayer. Most of the time, we would be better off asking for mercy, not justice.

Jeremiah 11:18–20
Psalm 7
John 7:40–53

Jesus told her, "I am the resurrection and the life; whoever believes in me, even if he dies, will live, and everyone who lives and believes in me will never die. Do you believe this?"

—JOHN 11:25–26

"Yes, Lord," Martha answered, but she still protested when Jesus wanted to roll away the stone covering her brother's tomb. She believed that Jesus was the promised Messiah, the Son of God—but she could not even begin to imagine how much power was available to him.

Ezekiel 37:12–14
Psalm 130
Romans 8:8–11
John 11:1–45 or 11:3–7, 17, 20–27, 33b–45

*"I am completely trapped," Susanna groaned. "If I yield, it will be my
death; if I refuse, I cannot escape your power. Yet it is better for me to
fall into your power without guilt than to sin before the Lord."*

—DANIEL 13:22–23

How human it is to justify doing something wrong when
doing the right thing means getting into trouble. And yet
Susanna chose to die rather than to give in to evil men.
She did not expect her story to have a happy ending.

Daniel 13:1–9, 15–17, 19–30, 33–62 or 13:41c–62
Psalm 23
John 8:1–11

From Mount Hor they set out on the Red Sea road, to bypass the land of Edom. But with their patience worn out by the journey, the people complained against God and Moses, "Why have you brought us up from Egypt to die in this desert, where there is no food or water? We are disgusted with this wretched food!"

—NUMBERS 21:4–5

It's easy to say they were ungrateful. After all, they were on a journey from slavery to freedom. God was providing food and water as they caravanned through the desert. But have you ever been so tired that you forgot your priorities and lost sight of your blessings?

Numbers 21:4–9
Psalm 102
John 8:21–30

Shadrach, Meshach, and Abednego answered King Nebuchadnezzar,
"There is no need for us to defend ourselves before you in this matter.
If our God, whom we serve, can save us from the white-hot furnace
and from your hands, O king, may he save us! But even if he will not,
know, O king, that we will not serve your god or worship the golden
statue which you set up."

—DANIEL 3:16–18

Some people lose their faith in God when things go
terribly wrong. These three young men had a different
kind of faith. They hoped God would save them from
death, but fear of death would not dissuade them from
trusting God.

Daniel 3:14–20, 91–92, 95
Daniel 3:52–56
John 8:31–42

I will maintain my covenant with you and your descendants after you throughout the ages as an everlasting pact, to be your God and the God of your descendants after you.

—GENESIS 17:7

God's promise to Abraham has been extended to us, the followers of Jesus. Mary sang of this promise in the Magnificat, her hymn of praise:

"He has helped Israel his servant,
remembering his mercy,
according to his promise to our fathers,
to Abraham and to his descendants forever."
(Luke 1:54–55)

Genesis 17:3–9
Psalm 105
John 8:51–59

*All those who were my friends
are on the watch for any misstep of mine.*

—JEREMIAH 20:10

Following God's direction, the prophet Jeremiah spoke out against his nation's corruption. He must have expected trouble from those in power, but why would his friends turn against him? Would God abandon him too? Though he wrote "the LORD is with me, like a mighty champion" (20:11), his anguish was profound. Read verses 7–18 and weep with him.

Jeremiah 20:10–13
Psalm 18
John 10:31–42

And when your time comes and you rest with your ancestors, I will raise up your heir after you, sprung from your loins, and I will make his kingdom firm.

—2 SAMUEL 7:12

God made this promise to King David almost a thousand years before the birth of Jesus, David's descendant. Jesus, often called "the son of David" in the New Testament, would make David's kingdom firm—by wearing a crown of thorns.

2 Samuel 7:4–5a, 12–14a, 16
Psalm 89
Romans 4:13, 16–18, 22
Matthew 1:16, 18–21, 24a or Luke 2:41–51a

Peter said to him, "Even though I should have to die with you, I will not deny you." And all the disciples spoke likewise.

—MATTHEW 26:35

The disciples were right to pledge their loyalty to Jesus, just as men and women are right to pledge their loyalty to each other in marriage. Yet Peter did deny Christ, and about one in five Roman Catholics have been divorced. Peter and all the rest of us are human. Our lives do not necessarily follow our plans. Fortunately, Christ offers grace and forgiveness.

Matthew 21:1–11
Isaiah 50:4–7
Psalm 22
Philippians 2:6–11
Matthew 26:14–27:66 or 27:11–54

I, the LORD, have called you for the victory of justice,
I have grasped you by the hand;
I formed you, and set you
as a covenant of the people,
a light for the nations.

—ISAIAH 42:6

As his time of suffering approached, Jesus must have found
strength in knowing that God had appointed him to bring
justice to the suffering human race.

Isaiah 42:1–7
Psalm 27
John 12:1–11

Though I thought I had toiled in vain,
and for nothing, uselessly, spent my strength,
Yet my reward is with the LORD,
my recompense is with my God.

—ISAIAH 49:4

We may live with integrity, sacrificing our own interests to help others, and still feel that we have accomplished nothing. Our reward may come not in our lifetime but long after we have died. It may happen on earth; it will certainly happen in heaven.

Isaiah 49:1–6
Psalm 71
John 13:21–33, 36–38

Wednesday

MARCH 19

I gave my back to those who beat me,
my cheeks to those who plucked my beard;
My face I did not shield
from buffets and spitting.

The Lord GOD is my help,
therefore I am not disgraced.

—ISAIAH 50:6–7

Tonight many parishes will celebrate the service of
Tenebrae, Latin for "darkness." Psalms will be chanted and
lamentations sung as Christ's suffering is recalled. Yet even
as darkness threatened to extinguish the light of the world,
Jesus knew that God was with him.

Isaiah 50:4–9a
Psalm 69
Matthew 26:14–25

Peter said to him, "You will never wash my feet." Jesus answered him,
"Unless I wash you, you will have no inheritance with me." Simon
Peter said to him, "Master, then not only my feet, but my hands and
head as well."

—JOHN 13:8–9

The usual homilies about this story tell us that Jesus'
disciples must willingly serve others. This is true, of course,
but the story also tells us that we must willingly be served.
Why is it often easier to serve than to be served?

Chrism Mass:
Isaiah 61:1–3a, 6a, 8b–9
Psalm 89
Revelation 1:5–8
Luke 4:16–21

Evening Mass of the Lord's Supper:
Exodus 12:1–8, 11–14
Psalm 116
1 Corinthians 11:23–26
John 13:1–15

Yet it was our infirmities that he bore,
our sufferings that he endured,
While we thought of him as stricken,
as one smitten by God and afflicted.
But he was pierced for our offenses,
crushed for our sins,
Upon him was the chastisement that makes us whole,
by his stripes we were healed.

—ISAIAH 53:4–5

It was not God's anger toward us that put Jesus on the cross; it was human sin, which by its very nature leads to death. God's love for us is so great that he voluntarily suffered in our place.

Isaiah 52:13–53:12
Psalm 31
Hebrews 4:14–16; 5:7–9
John 18:1–19:42

Saturday

MARCH 22

• HOLY SATURDAY •

Then {Mary Magdalene and the other Mary} went away quickly from the tomb, fearful yet overjoyed, and ran to announce this to his disciples. And behold, Jesus met them on their way and greeted them.

—MATTHEW 28:8–9

After experiencing "a great earthquake" and a message from "an angel of the Lord" who looked like lightning (28:2–3), the women were terrified. But they did not let their fear stop them. They ran to announce the good news anyway—and in the midst of their terror, they met the resurrected Jesus.

Genesis 1:1–2:2 or 1:1, 26–31a
Psalm 104 or 33
Genesis 22:1–18 or 22:1–2, 9a, 10–13, 15–18
Psalm 16
Exodus 14:15–15:1
Exodus 15:1–6, 17–18
Isaiah 54:5–14
Psalm 30
Isaiah 55:1–11
Isaiah 12:2–6
Baruch 3:9–15, 32–4:4
Psalm 19
Ezekiel 36:16–17a, 18–28
Psalm 42; 43 or Isaiah 12:2–3, 4bcd, 5–6 or Psalm 51
Romans 6:3–11
Psalm 118
Matthew 28:1–10

If then you were raised with Christ, seek what is above,
where Christ is seated at the right hand of God. Think of what is above,
not of what is on earth. For you have died, and your life is hidden
with Christ in God. When Christ your life appears, then you too
will appear with him in glory.

—COLOSSIANS 3:1–4

Now that Christ has been raised to new life, death can never touch him again. When we realize that "in Christ shall all be brought to life" (1 Corinthians 15:22), we lose our fear of death. We are safe in Christ's care, knowing that death cannot hold us any more than it held him.

Acts 10:34a, 37–43
Psalm 118
Colossians 3:1–4 or 1 Corinthians 5:6b–8
John 20:1–9 or Matthew 28:1–10 or, at an afternoon or evening Mass, Luke 24:13–35

God raised this Jesus; of this we are all witnesses.

—ACTS 2:32

Peter's listeners were inclined to believe his assertion. In the fifty days since Jesus' resurrection, reports of Jesus sightings had been widespread. Some twenty years later, Paul would write that over five hundred people saw the risen Christ (1 Corinthians 15:5–8). It was hard to doubt that Christ had been raised from the dead—even though it seemed impossible—because there were so many witnesses.

Acts 2:14, 22–33
Psalm 16
Matthew 28:8–15

MARCH 25

"Therefore let the whole house of Israel know for certain that God has made him both Lord and Messiah, this Jesus whom you crucified."

Now when they heard this, they were cut to the heart, and they asked Peter and the other apostles, "What are we to do, my brothers?"

—ACTS 2:36–37

Head, heart, and hand—the three work together in an authentic faith experience. What is the truth? How does it make us feel? What should we do about it?

Acts 2:36–41
Psalm 33
John 20:11–18

When he saw Peter and John about to go into the temple, he asked for alms. But Peter looked intently at him, as did John, and said, "Look at us." He paid attention to them, expecting to receive something from them. Peter said, "I have neither silver nor gold, but what I do have I give you: in the name of Jesus Christ the Nazorean, [rise and] walk."

—ACTS 3:3–6

What do you need from God in order to get through the day? Go ahead and ask for it—and don't be surprised if you get something better.

Acts 3:1–10
Psalm 105
Luke 24:13–35

The author of life you put to death, but God raised him from the dead;
of this we are witnesses. And by faith in his name, this man, whom
you see and know, his name has made strong, and the faith that comes
through it has given him this perfect health, in the presence of all of you.

—ACTS 3:15–16

Everyone in Jerusalem knew that Jesus had been a powerful
healer, but Jesus was dead. If it was amazing to see Peter
and John heal a crippled beggar, it was downright alarming
to hear that their power came from Jesus. Maybe some of
the onlookers had yelled for Jesus' crucifixion just a few
weeks ago. Now they were witnessing his power at work.
Was there something about Jesus they hadn't suspected?

Acts 3:11–26
Psalm 8
Luke 24:35–48

There is no salvation through anyone else, nor is there any other name under heaven given to the human race by which we are to be saved.

—ACTS 4:12

Maybe someone has asked you, "Are you saved?" What does *salvation* mean? In Scripture, it often means being restored to wholeness or healed. It can apply to the body as well as the soul; in fact, true wholeness has to include both. The best answer to "Are you saved?" is "I am being saved." Ultimately, Jesus will completely restore us, body and soul.

Acts 4:1–12
Psalm 118
John 21:1–14

Peter and John, however, said to them in reply, "Whether it is right in the sight of God for us to obey you rather than God, you be the judges. . . ." After threatening them further, they released them, finding no way to punish them, on account of the people who were all praising God for what had happened.

—ACTS 4:19, 21

Peter, today the symbol of ultimate human authority in the Catholic Church, constantly irritated the powerful religious authorities of his day. Powerful people often threaten others because they feel threatened themselves.

Acts 4:13–21
Psalm 118
Mark 16:9–15

On the evening of that first day of the week, when the doors were locked, where the disciples were, for fear of the Jews, Jesus came and stood in their midst and said to them, "Peace be with you."

—JOHN 20:19

How peaceful would you feel if you had bolted your doors, locked your windows, and activated your alarm system—and suddenly someone whose funeral you had just attended strode into your living room?

Acts 2:42–47
Psalm 118
1 Peter 1:3–9
John 20:19–31

Mary said, "Behold, I am the handmaid of the Lord. May it be done to me according to your word."

—LUKE 1:38

What the angel proposed was impossible (yes, Mary knew where babies come from) and would certainly compromise Mary's reputation (Joseph also had a good grip on biology). But Mary still found joy in obedience: "{M}y spirit rejoices in God my savior," she sang. "{F}rom now on will all ages call me blessed" (Luke 1:47–48).

Isaiah 7:10–14; 8:10
Psalm 93
Hebrews 10:4–10
Luke 1:26–38

The community of believers was of one heart and mind, and no one claimed that any of his possessions was his own, but they had everything in common. . . . There was no needy person among them, for those who owned property or houses would sell them, bring the proceeds of the sale, and put them at the feet of the apostles, and they were distributed to each according to need.

—ACTS 4:32, 34–35

American Catholics, on average, contribute less than 1.5 percent of their household income to their parish.

Acts 4:32–37
Psalm 93
John 3:7b–15

But the court officers who went did not find them in the prison, so they came back and reported, "We found the jail securely locked and the guards stationed outside the doors, but when we opened them, we found no one inside."

—ACTS 5:22–23

Just as the disciples could not lock the risen Jesus out (John 20:19), the authorities could not lock the Spirit-filled disciples in.

Acts 5:17–26
Psalm 34
John 3:16–21

But Peter and the apostles said in reply, "We must obey God rather than men."

—ACTS 5:29

How did Peter and the apostles know that God was not speaking through the high priest? How can we tell the difference between God's laws and human laws?

Acts 5:27–33
Psalm 34
John 3:31–36

{H}ave nothing to do with these men, and let them go. For if this endeavor or this activity is of human origin, it will destroy itself. But if it comes from God, you will not be able to destroy them; you may even find yourselves fighting against God.

—ACTS 5:38–39

This advice from Rabbi Gamaliel (whose most famous student was later known as St. Paul) is good to remember whenever we're inclined to judge new and unsettling ideas. Give them time and see what develops.

Acts 5:34–42
Psalm 27
John 6:1–15

At that time, as the number of disciples continued to grow, the Hellenists complained against the Hebrews because their widows were being neglected in the daily distribution.

—ACTS 6:1

The early church was full of the Holy Spirit's power and grew rapidly. Being composed of human beings, however, it was not perfect. Still, this dispute between Greek-speaking and Hebrew-speaking members had a happy outcome. To meet the church's increasing needs, the office of deacon was created.

Acts 6:1–7
Psalm 33
John 6:16–21

And it happened that while they were conversing and debating, Jesus himself drew near and walked with them, but their eyes were prevented from recognizing him.

—LUKE 24:15–16

The two disciples on their way to Emmaus finally recognized Jesus when "he took bread, said the blessing, broke it, and gave it to them" (24:30). As we receive communion today, let us recognize Jesus in the broken bread, and as we go about our daily work this week, let us recognize that Jesus is walking with us.

Acts 2:14, 22–23
Psalm 16
1 Peter 1:17–21
Luke 24:13–35

Monday

APRIL 7

• ST. JOHN BAPTIST DE LA SALLE, PRIEST •

All those who sat in the Sanhedrin looked intently at him and saw that his face was like the face of an angel.

—ACTS 6:15

The Sanhedrin was the nation's seventy-one-member supreme court. Stephen, one of the first seven deacons, was on trial for his life, and the witnesses for the prosecution were lying about him. What emotions would you expect him to show? How would you picture "the face of an angel"? What could account for his appearance?

Acts 6:8–15
Psalm 119
John 6:22–29

The witnesses laid down their cloaks at the feet of a young man named Saul. As they were stoning Stephen, he called out, "Lord Jesus, receive my spirit." Then he fell to his knees and cried out in a loud voice, "Lord, do not hold this sin against them"; and when he said this, he fell asleep.

—ACTS 7:58–60

Young Saul had not seen Jesus dying on the cross, but he heard Stephen's dying words, which echoed the last words of Jesus (see Luke 23:34, 46). Though Saul was an enemy of the church, he must have been deeply affected by Stephen's martyrdom. In a few years, Saul would become Paul, the apostle to the Gentiles.

Acts 7:51–8:1a
Psalm 31
John 6:30–35

APRIL 9

On that day, there broke out a severe persecution of the church in Jerusalem, and all were scattered throughout the countryside of Judea and Samaria, except the apostles. . . .

Now those who had been scattered went about preaching the word.
—ACTS 8:1, 4

"The oftener we are mown down by you,
the more in number we grow; the blood of Christians
is seed" (Tertullian).

Acts 8:1b–8
Psalm 66
John 6:35–40

*Philip ran up and heard him reading Isaiah the prophet and said,
"Do you understand what you are reading?" He replied, "How can I,
unless someone instructs me?" . . . Then Philip opened his mouth and,
beginning with this scripture passage, he proclaimed Jesus to him.*

—ACTS 8:30–31, 35

Do you belong to a Bible study group? If your parish offers
one, consider signing up, or start one with friends. The
Bible somehow becomes clearer and more personal when it
is shared.

Acts 8:26–40
Psalm 66
John 6:44–51

Now Saul, still breathing murderous threats against the disciples of the Lord, went to the high priest and asked him for letters to the synagogues in Damascus, that, if he should find any men or women who belonged to the Way, he might bring them back to Jerusalem in chains.

—ACTS 9:1–2

Saul eagerly volunteered to help root out the new sect. Damascus is 135 miles from Jerusalem, a journey of several days on foot or horseback, but the long distance did not faze Saul. Apparently God liked his enthusiasm, even though Saul was headed in entirely the wrong direction. This, after all, is the beginning of his conversion story.

Acts 9:1–20
Psalm 117
John 6:52–59

{T}hey took {Peter} to the room upstairs where all the widows came to him weeping and showing him the tunics and cloaks that Dorcas had made while she was with them.

—ACTS 9:39

Dorcas had died. When Peter came and prayed, she came back to life. "This became known all over Joppa, and many came to believe in the Lord" (9:42). Was it the miracle that caused people to believe? Or was it the startling realization that Christians, like Dorcas, really cared for the poor and suffering?

Acts 9:31–42
Psalm 116
John 6:60–69

Amen, amen, I say to you, whoever does not enter a sheepfold through the gate but climbs over elsewhere is a thief and a robber. But whoever enters through the gate is the shepherd of the sheep. . . .

I am the gate.

—JOHN 10:1–2, 9

Today, just as in the ancient world, many religions compete for followers. With hundreds of choices available and new religions constantly springing up, how can a person know what to believe and whom to follow?

Acts 2:14a, 36–41
Psalm 23
1 Peter 2:20b–25
John 10:1–10

Monday

APRIL 14

"As I began to speak, the holy Spirit fell upon them as it had upon us at the beginning. . . . If then God gave them the same gift he gave to us when we came to believe in the Lord Jesus Christ, who was I to be able to hinder God?" When they heard this, they stopped objecting and glorified God, saying, "God has then granted life-giving repentance to the Gentiles too."

—ACTS 11:15, 17–18

We tend to think of repentance as something we do, and if we do it right, God forgives us. But "life-giving repentance" is a gift from God. God always reaches out to us before we reach out to God.

Acts 11:1–18
Psalm 42
John 10:11–18

Now those who had been scattered by the persecution that arose because of Stephen went as far as Phoenicia, Cyprus, and Antioch, preaching the word to no one but Jews. There were some Cypriots and Cyrenians among them, however, who came to Antioch and began to speak to the Greeks as well. . . . {I}t was in Antioch that the disciples were first called Christians.

—ACTS 11:19–20, 26

It is significant that the word *Christian* was first used in one of the first cities where Jews and Greeks (Gentiles) came together to worship. Disciples can come from any background. The Christian faith is open to everybody.

Acts 11:19–26
Psalm 87
John 10:22–30

While they were worshiping the Lord and fasting, the holy Spirit said,
"Set apart for me Barnabas and Saul for the work to which I have
called them." Then, completing their fasting and prayer, they laid hands
on them and sent them off.

—ACTS 13:2–3

Thus began the Christian mission to the world. In just
a few years, the gospel of Jesus Christ would be known
throughout the Roman Empire. When people—even a
small number of them—fast and pray and listen to the
Holy Spirit, the results can be amazing.

Acts 12:24–13:5a
Psalm 67
John 12:44–50

So Paul got up, motioned with his hand, and said, "Fellow Israelites and you others who are God-fearing, listen. The God of this people Israel chose our ancestors and exalted the people during their sojourn in the land of Egypt."

—ACTS 13:16−17

This is the beginning of a homily showing Jesus as the promised descendant of Israel's greatest king, David. Christianity is solidly built on a Jewish foundation. To learn more about your Christian faith, study the Old Testament.

Acts 13:13−25
Psalm 89
John 13:16−20

But God raised him from the dead, and for many days he appeared to those who had come up with him from Galilee to Jerusalem. These are [now] his witnesses before the people.

—ACTS 13:30–31

Paul proclaims here the heart of the gospel: Jesus was dead, and now he lives. Everything that the church teaches and practices flows from this central, almost unbelievable Good News.

Acts 13:26–33
Psalm 2
John 14:1–6

The disciples were filled with joy and the holy Spirit.

—ACTS 13:52

This is the surprising conclusion to a story in which Paul and Barnabas were rejected, persecuted, and kicked out of town. Despite fierce opposition, many people—both Jews and Gentiles—had become disciples. They could see that following Jesus did not lead to comfort or popularity. Why were they joyful?

Acts 13:44–52
Psalm 98
John 14:7–14

Do not let your hearts be troubled. You have faith in God; have faith also in me. In my Father's house there are many dwelling places. If there were not, would I have told you that I am going to prepare a place for you? And if I go and prepare a place for you, I will come back again and take you to myself, so that where I am you also may be.

—JOHN 14:1–3

For a few years, "the Word became flesh / and made his dwelling among us" (John 1:14). Now he is preparing dwelling places for us, where we will be with him forever. "Christ has died, Christ is risen, Christ will come again."

Acts 6:1–7
Psalm 33
1 Peter 2:4–9
John 14:1–12

When the crowds saw what Paul had done, they cried out . . . "The gods have come down to us in human form." . . .

The apostles Barnabas and Paul tore their garments . . . , shouting, "Men, why are you doing this? We are of the same nature as you, human beings."

—ACTS 14:11, 14–15

"Those who are in a position to help others will realize that in doing so they themselves receive help; being able to help others is no merit or achievement of their own. This duty is a grace. . . . We recognize that we are not acting on the basis of any superiority or greater personal efficiency, but because the Lord has graciously enabled us to do so" (Pope Benedict XVI).

Acts 14:5–18
Psalm 115
John 14:21–26

They strengthened the spirits of the disciples and exhorted them to persevere in the faith, saying, "It is necessary for us to undergo many hardships to enter the kingdom of God."

—ACTS 14:22

How does your Christian faith make your life more difficult?

Acts 14:19–28
Psalm 145
John 14:27–31a

Some who had come down from Judea were instructing the brothers,
"Unless you are circumcised according to the Mosaic practice, you
cannot be saved."

—ACTS 15:1

The Judeans were devout and meant well, but they had
a narrow view of salvation. Warning bells should ring
whenever we hear someone say, "Unless you do this [or "If
you do that"], you cannot be saved." God's mercy is wider
than ours.

Acts 15:1–6
Psalm 122
John 15:1–8

Thursday

APRIL 24

Why, then, are you now putting God to the test by placing on the shoulders of the disciples a yoke that neither our ancestors nor we have been able to bear? On the contrary, we believe that we are saved through the grace of the Lord Jesus, in the same way as they.

—ACTS 15:10–11

It is one thing for me to accept strict discipline for myself, quite another to impose it on others—especially since the Christian faith is built on God's grace, not human actions.

Acts 15:7–21
Psalm 96
John 15:9–11

Friday

APRIL 25

*He said to them, "Go into the whole world and proclaim the gospel to
every creature."*

—MARK 16:15

The world's population was about 300 million when the
Gospel of Mark was written. Today it is twenty times
larger—some 6.5 billion. How can "every creature" hear
the Good News? As Jesus told the disciples in another
difficult situation, "For human beings it is impossible, but
not for God. All things are possible for God" (Mark 10:27).

1 Peter 5:5b–14
Psalm 89
Mark 16:15–20

They traveled through the Phrygian and Galatian territory because they had been prevented by the holy Spirit from preaching the message in the province of Asia. When they came to Mysia, they tried to go on into Bithynia, but the Spirit of Jesus did not allow them.

—ACTS 16:6–7

Why is it that when things go wrong and my plans get all messed up, it never occurs to me that the Holy Spirit may be involved?

Acts 16:1–10
Psalm 100
John 15:18–21

I will not leave you orphans; I will come to you.

—JOHN 14:18

"I am with you." This was God's assurance to the patriarchs
Isaac and Jacob; to Joshua, who led God's people into the
Promised Land; and to the people of Israel, even during
times of discouragement and defeat. It was Jesus' promise
to his disciples as he commissioned them to preach and
baptize, and to Paul as he preached his way through the
Roman Empire. In fact, the name Emmanuel means "God is
with us." God never leaves us orphans.

Acts 8:5–8, 14–17
Psalm 66
1 Peter 3:15–18
John 14:15–21

Monday

APRIL 28

• ST. PETER CHANEL, PRIEST AND MARTYR • ST. LOUIS MARY DE
MONTFORT, PRIEST •

*{A} woman named Lydia, a dealer in purple cloth, . . . listened, and the
Lord opened her heart to pay attention to what Paul was saying. After
she and her household had been baptized, she offered us an invitation,
"If you consider me a believer in the Lord, come and stay at my home,"
and she prevailed on us.*

—ACTS 16:14–15

Thanks to the hospitality of a busy working mother, a
Christian church was established in Philippi.

Acts 16:11–15
Psalm 149
John 15:26–16:4a

Tuesday

APRIL 29

• ST. CATHERINE OF SIENA, VIRGIN AND DOCTOR OF THE CHURCH •

When the jailer woke up and saw the prison doors wide open, he drew [his] sword and was about to kill himself, thinking that the prisoners had escaped. But Paul shouted out in a loud voice, "Do no harm to yourself; we are all here."

—ACTS 16:27–28

If you were the jailer, would you have rushed to punish yourself in this situation, or would you have pointed the finger at someone or something else? Why does taking personal responsibility seem so peculiar?

Acts 16:22–34
Psalm 138
John 16:5–11

Then Paul stood up at the Areopagus and said:

"You Athenians, I see that in every respect you are very religious. For as I walked around looking carefully at your shrines, I even discovered an altar inscribed, 'To an Unknown God.' What therefore you unknowingly worship, I proclaim to you."

—ACTS 17:22–23

Like the Athenians, we often need reminding that God is not a human invention or a vague force: he is our Creator and Judge.

Acts 17:15, 22–18:1
Psalm 148
John 16:12–15

May the eyes of [your] hearts be enlightened, that you may know . . .
what is the surpassing greatness of his power for us who believe, in
accord with the exercise of his great might, which he worked in Christ,
raising him from the dead and seating him at his right hand in the
heavens, far above every principality, authority, power,
and dominion, and every name that is named not only in this age
but also in the one to come.

—EPHESIANS 1:18–21

What is the meaning of the Ascension? That the whole
universe is being ruled by the One who died for us.

Acts 1:1–11
Psalm 47
Ephesians 1:17–23
Matthew 28:16–20

Friday

MAY 2

One night in a vision the Lord said to Paul, "Do not be afraid. Go on speaking, and do not be silent, for I am with you. No one will attack and harm you, for I have many people in this city." He settled there for a year and a half and taught the word of God among them.

—ACTS 18:9–11

It can seem hard to speak up for what is right, to defend Christian beliefs, even to identify oneself as a Christian. But what exactly are we afraid of? Even if our fear is realistic, is it a reason to remain silent?

Acts 18:9–18
Psalm 47
John 16:20–23

Philip said to him, "Master, show us the Father, and that will be enough for us."

—JOHN 14:8

Back when Philip decided to become Jesus' disciple, Philip's friend Nathanael was skeptical. "Come and see," Philip said (John 1:46). For Philip, seeing was believing—but he had not yet really grasped who Jesus was. "Whoever has seen me has seen the Father," Jesus told him (14:9).

1 Corinthians 15:1–8
Psalm 19
John 14:6–14

*I glorified you on earth by accomplishing the work
that you gave me to do. . . .*

*And now I will no longer be in the world, but they are in the world,
while I am coming to you.*

—JOHN 17:4, 11

The ten days between Jesus' ascension and the gift
of the Holy Spirit at Pentecost must have seemed long
and bleak to the disciples. What did it mean that Jesus
had gone to his Father (see John 20:17)? Were they on
their own now? Who was the Advocate whom Jesus had
promised to send (John 16:7)?

Acts 1:12–14
Psalm 27
1 Peter 4:13–16
John 17:1–11a

*He said to them, "Did you receive the holy Spirit when you became
believers?" They answered him, "We have never even heard that there is
a holy Spirit." He said, "How were you baptized?" They replied, "With
the baptism of John."*

—ACTS 19:2–3

John's baptism was for repentance and conversion. The
baptism of the Holy Spirit is for the power to carry out
Jesus' mission on earth. Christian baptism incorporates
both: "Through Baptism we are freed from sin and reborn
as sons of God; we become members of Christ, are
incorporated into the Church and made sharers in her
mission" (*Catechism of the Catholic Church,* 1213).

Acts 19:1–8
Psalm 68
John 16:29–33

But now, compelled by the Spirit, I am going to Jerusalem. What will happen to me there I do not know, except that in one city after another the holy Spirit has been warning me that imprisonment and hardships await me.

—ACTS 20:22–23

I don't know—nor do I want to know—how or when I will die. But I do know that someday death will come, and very few deaths are painless. Will I be terrified? Or will I go calmly, like Paul, considering "life of no importance to me, if only I may finish . . . the ministry that I received from the Lord Jesus" (20:24)?

Acts 20:17–27
Psalm 68
John 17:1–11a

I know that after my departure savage wolves will come among you, and they will not spare the flock. And from your own group, men will come forward perverting the truth to draw the disciples away after them. So be vigilant.

—ACTS 20:29–31

Not everyone who claims to speak in God's name has good intentions. Not everyone who writes or speaks about religion teaches Christian truth. It isn't always easy to know which religious leaders to believe. One way to tell is to look at how they measure up to Jesus. Do they teach as he did? Live as he did? Love as he did?

Acts 20:28–38
Psalm 68
John 17:11b–19

Thursday

MAY 8

The dispute was so serious that the commander, afraid that Paul would be torn to pieces by them, ordered his troops to go down and rescue him. . . . The following night the Lord stood by him and said, "Take courage. For just as you have borne witness to my cause in Jerusalem, so you must also bear witness in Rome."

—ACTS 23:10–11

Neither Jerusalem nor Rome was safe for Paul. In both cities he was imprisoned; in one he would be killed. If Paul had valued personal safety more than his assignment from God, what would have happened to the young Christian church?

Acts 22:30; 23:6–11
Psalm 16
John 17:20–26

His accusers stood around him, but did not charge him with any of the crimes I suspected. Instead they had some issues with him about their own religion and about a certain Jesus who had died but who Paul claimed was alive.

—ACTS 25:18–19

Festus, the Roman procurator, was mystified.
The religious authorities wanted Paul condemned, but
Festus could not find any reason to put him to death.
Paul said strange things about voices from the sky and a
Messiah who rose from the dead (see Acts 26), but he was
not guilty of any crime.

Acts 25:13b–21
Psalm 103
John 21:15–19

When he entered Rome, Paul was allowed to live by himself, with the soldier who was guarding him. . . .

He remained for two full years in his lodgings. He received all who came to him, and with complete assurance and without hindrance he proclaimed the kingdom of God and taught about the Lord Jesus Christ.
—ACTS 28:16, 30–31

The book of Acts ends right there, with no further information about Paul. That's probably because the book isn't really about Paul—or Peter or any other person. It's about the Holy Spirit working through the church to proclaim Jesus' kingdom "to the ends of the earth" (Acts 1:8). Once Paul was preaching in Rome, that mission was accomplished.

Acts 28:16–20, 30–31
Psalm 11
John 21:20–25

When the time for Pentecost was fulfilled, they were all in one place together.

—ACTS 2:1

Seven weeks had gone by since Jesus' resurrection. Rather than giving up and going home, his friends stayed together and prayed. Suddenly the Spirit "came to rest on each one of them" (2:3), and they went out and preached to another group of people who had come together to pray—"devout Jews from every nation under heaven staying in Jerusalem" (2:5). When God's people pray together, God's power is released in the world.

Vigil:	**Day:**
Genesis 11:1–9 or Exodus 19:3–8a, 16–20b	Acts 2:1–11
or Ezekiel 37:1–14 or Joel 3:1–5	Psalm 104
Psalm 104	1 Corinthians 12:3b–7, 12–13
Romans 8:22–27	John 20:19–23
John 7:37–39	

Monday

MAY 12

• ST. NEREUS, ST. ACHILLEUS, AND ST. PANCRAS, MARTYRS •

Consider it all joy, my brothers, when you encounter various trials, for you know that the testing of your faith produces perseverance.

—JAMES 1:2–3

"What does not destroy me, makes me stronger" (Friedrich Nietzsche).

James 1:1–11
Psalm 119
Mark 8:11–13

No one experiencing temptation should say, "I am being tempted by God"; for God is not subject to temptation to evil, and he himself tempts no one. Rather, each person is tempted when he is lured and enticed by his own desire.

—JAMES 1:13–14

In Buddhism, desire is the source of suffering. In Christianity, desire for what we should not have is the source of sin. But not all desire is bad. Desire for what we should have—and have been given through God's grace—is the source of thanksgiving.

James 1:12–18
Psalm 94
Mark 8:14–21

Wednesday

MAY 14

• ST. MATTHIAS, APOSTLE •

{I}t is necessary that one of the men who accompanied us the whole time the Lord Jesus came and went among us, beginning from the baptism of John until the day on which he was taken up from us, become with us a witness to his resurrection.

—ACTS 1:21–22

As I write this, America is at war. This weekend, yet another foreign correspondent was seriously injured. On TV this morning, someone asked a reporter how journalists can constantly risk their lives in such dangerous places. "Because," the reporter answered, "someone has to bear witness."

Acts 1:15–17, 20–26
Psalm 113
John 15:9–17

⇒ 167 ⇐

{I}f a man with gold rings on his fingers and in fine clothes comes into your assembly, and a poor person in shabby clothes also comes in, and you pay attention to the one wearing the fine clothes and say, "Sit here, please," while you say to the poor one, "Stand there," or "Sit at my feet," have you not made distinctions among yourselves and become judges with evil designs?

—JAMES 2:2–4

Or maybe we make snap judgments based on the person's accent, or skin color, or mannerisms, or weight, or . . .

James 2:1–9
Psalm 34
Mark 8:27–33

*If a brother or sister has nothing to wear and has no food for the day,
and one of you says to them, "Go in peace, keep warm, and eat well,"
but you do not give them the necessities of the body, what good is it?*

—JAMES 2:15–16

Of course we wish people well. On TV we see desolate,
worn-out refugees; starving children with distended bellies;
destitute survivors of earthquakes and tsunamis. We weep
in sympathy. But what do we do to help them?

James 2:14–24, 26
Psalm 112
Mark 8:34–9:1

Saturday

MAY 17

For every kind of beast and bird, of reptile and sea creature, can be tamed and has been tamed by the human species, but no human being can tame the tongue. It is a restless evil, full of deadly poison.

—JAMES 3:7–8

If that sounds extreme, pay close attention to what your tongue does today.

James 3:1–10
Psalm 12
Mark 9:2–13

For God so loved the world that he gave his only Son, so that everyone who believes in him might not perish but might have eternal life. For God did not send his Son into the world to condemn the world, but that the world might be saved through him.

—JOHN 3:16–17

Which of these statements are common beliefs? Which statement is true?

"God is angry with the world."

"Jesus died to protect us from God's rage."

"Just in case God is having a bad day, we are safer praying through Jesus or Mary or one of the saints."

"God loves the world and wants to save us from the mess we've gotten ourselves into."

Exodus 34:4b–6, 8–9
Daniel 3:52–56
2 Corinthians 13:11–13
John 3:16–18

For where jealousy and selfish ambition exist, there is disorder and every foul practice. But the wisdom from above is first of all pure, then peaceable, gentle, compliant, full of mercy and good fruits, without inconstancy or insincerity. And the fruit of righteousness is sown in peace for those who cultivate peace.

—JAMES 3:16–18

Toward the end of America's involvement in Vietnam, representatives of the warring parties met in Paris to discuss peace. Negotiations were postponed for several months, however, as diplomats argued fiercely about logistics, including the shape of the negotiating table (round? rectangular?). Not surprisingly, the Nobel Prize–winning Paris Peace Accords broke down less than two years after being signed.

James 3:13–18
Psalm 19
Mark 9:14–29

You covet but do not possess. You kill and envy but you cannot obtain;
you fight and wage war.

—JAMES 4:2

Billions of dollars are spent every year to induce us to
covet products and to believe that if we buy the right
ones we will be happier, prettier, healthier, sexier. And last
year's products won't do. We lose status if we go out of
date—and anyway, don't we want the economy to grow?
The trouble is that so many of the resources we need come
from other countries. What will we do if we can't get them
by peaceful means?

James 4:1–10
Psalm 55
Mark 9:30–37

• ST. CHRISTOPHER MAGALLANES, PRIEST AND MARTYR, AND HIS
COMPANIONS, MARTYRS •

*Come now, you who say, "Today or tomorrow we shall go into such
and such a town, spend a year there doing business, and make a
profit"—you have no idea what your life will be like tomorrow. You are
a puff of smoke that appears briefly and then disappears.*

—JAMES 4:13–14

My neighbor was excited. She had just retired, and in days
she and her husband and two friends would be leaving for
a long-dreamed-of vacation in China. On the Saturday
morning after her last workday, she sat up in bed and said
to her husband, "I have the worst headache . . ." Those
were her last words.

James 4:13–17
Psalm 49
Mark 9:38–40

Thursday

MAY 22

Behold, the wages you withheld from the workers who harvested your fields are crying aloud, and the cries of the harvesters have reached the ears of the Lord of hosts. You have lived on earth in luxury and pleasure; you have fattened your hearts for the day of slaughter.

—JAMES 5:4–5

Whole grains, olive oil, fish, red wine—these wonderful foods help protect us from the fats that could damage our physical hearts. What can protect us from fattening our spiritual hearts for the day of slaughter, the day when we realize how much our pleasures have cost others?

James 5:1–6
Psalm 49
Mark 9:41–50

Friday

MAY 23

But above all, my brothers, do not swear, either by heaven or by earth or with any other oath, but let your "Yes" mean "Yes" and your "No" mean "No," that you may not incur condemnation.

—JAMES 5:12

Perjury—lying under oath—is a serious crime. But is it morally any worse than lying when one is not under oath? Truth is the foundation of justice, whether in court or in everyday life.

James 5:9–12
Psalm 103
Mark 10:1–12

Therefore, confess your sins to one another and pray for one another, that you may be healed. The fervent prayer of a righteous person is very powerful.

—JAMES 5:16

Because human beings are an indivisible union of body and soul, healing includes both the forgiveness of sins and the restoration of bodily health. In heaven, when our healing is complete, we will have bodies that do not decay united with souls that do not sin.

James 5:13–20
Psalm 141
Mark 10:13–16

The cup of blessing that we bless, is it not a participation in the blood of Christ? The bread that we break, is it not a participation in the body of Christ?

—1 CORINTHIANS 10:16

"As he revealed himself to the apostles in true flesh, so he reveals himself to us now in sacred bread. . . . Let us, as we see bread and wine with our bodily eyes, see and firmly believe that they are his most holy body and blood, living and true. And in this way the Lord is always with his faithful" (St. Francis of Assisi).

Deuteronomy 8:2–3, 14b–16a
Psalm 147
1 Corinthians 10:16–17
John 6:51–58

Monday

MAY 26

• ST. PHILIP NERI, PRIEST • MEMORIAL DAY •

Although you have not seen him you love him; even though you do not see him now yet believe in him, you rejoice with an indescribable and glorious joy, as you attain the goal of [your] faith, the salvation of your souls.

—1 PETER 1:8–9

We have not seen him, but his Spirit lives in us. We have not seen him, but his body and blood nourish us. We have not seen him, but we are his body.

1 Peter 1:3–9
Psalm 111
Mark 10:17–27

Like obedient children, do not act in compliance with the desires of your former ignorance but, as he who called you is holy, be holy yourselves in every aspect of your conduct.

—1 PETER 1:14–15

Remember when teenagers wore WWJD bracelets? Most probably didn't know that the acronym for "What would Jesus do?" came from an 1896 novel, *In His Steps*. When the characters in the novel start asking themselves the question, their lives are transformed—and so are the lives of the hungry, poor, and homeless people whom they realize Jesus would help.

1 Peter 1:10–16
Psalm 98
Mark 10:28–31

*You have been born anew, not from perishable but from imperishable
seed, through the living and abiding word of God.*

—1 PETER 1:23

A friend of mine was upset that her sister-in-law had
become "one of those born-agains." My friend associated
the term with a style of Christianity that she didn't like,
but in Scripture we learn that all Christians are born
again—including my friend. Jesus said, "{N}o one can enter
the kingdom of God without being born of water and
Spirit" (John 3:5). As Christians, we have been reborn to a
new and never-ending life.

1 Peter 1:18–25
Psalm 147
Mark 10:32–45

Maintain good conduct among the Gentiles, so that if they speak of you as evildoers, they may observe your good works and glorify God on the day of visitation.

—1 PETER 2:12

Jesus told his followers to judge prophets by the results of their words and actions: "By their fruits you will know them" (Matthew 7:16). As Christians, we are to be judged in the same way. Do our words and actions lead to war or to peace? To compassionate care or to increased poverty? To justice or to abuse? If we get bad press, what can we do about it?

1 Peter 2:2–5, 9–12
Psalm 100
Mark 10:46–52

It was not because you are the largest of all nations that the LORD set his heart on you and chose you, for you are really the smallest of all nations. It was because the LORD loved you and because of his fidelity to the oath he had sworn to your fathers.

—DEUTERONOMY 7:7–8

God doesn't love us because we're important. He loves us just as we are.

Deuteronomy 7:6–11
Psalm 103
1 John 4:7–16
Matthew 11:25–30

Blessed are you who believed that what was spoken to you by the Lord would be fulfilled.

—LUKE 1:45

Belief is not for the fainthearted. Mary, an unmarried teenager, believed the angel and became pregnant. Joseph, her fiancé, feared he would have to break up with her, and we can only imagine what her parents feared. Mary must have been surprised and relieved when she arrived at her cousin's house and Elizabeth greeted her by saying, "Most blessed are you among women" (1:42).

Zephaniah 3:14–18a or Romans 12:9–16
Isaiah 12:2–6
Luke 1:39–56

Many will say to me on that day, "Lord, Lord, did we not prophesy in your name? Did we not drive out demons in your name? Did we not do mighty deeds in your name?" Then I will declare to them solemnly, "I never knew you. Depart from me, you evildoers."

—MATTHEW 7:22–23

Why would Jesus reject people who had done great things in his name? Because they did not do "the will of my Father in heaven" (7:21). In violation of the second commandment ("You shall not take the name of the LORD, your God, in vain"—Exodus 20:7), they took the Lord's name and then disobeyed him.

Deuteronomy 11:18, 26–28, 32
Psalm 31
Romans 3:21–25, 28
Matthew 7:21–27

{M}ake every effort to supplement your faith with virtue, virtue with knowledge, knowledge with self-control, self-control with endurance, endurance with devotion, devotion with mutual affection, mutual affection with love.

—2 PETER 1:5–7

Do you know somebody who is faithful, reliable, wise, self-controlled, hardworking, devout, friendly, and self-sacrificing? Those words should describe every mature Christian. They do, in fact, perfectly describe my father-in-law, and today is his eighty-seventh birthday. Happy birthday, Dad!

2 Peter 1:2–7
Psalm 91
Mark 12:1–12

{On the day of God} the heavens will be dissolved in flames and the elements melted by fire. But according to his promise we await new heavens and a new earth in which righteousness dwells.

—2 PETER 3:12–13

Christians believe that Jesus has conquered death. With the coming of "a new heaven and a new earth," the cycle of death and rebirth will pass away, and "there shall be no more death or mourning, wailing or pain" (Revelation 21:1, 4).

2 Peter 3:12–15a, 17–18
Psalm 90
Mark 12:13–17

I know him in whom I have believed and am confident that he is able to guard what has been entrusted to me until that day.

—2 TIMOTHY 1:12

Paul's life was nearly over; soon he would be executed. There are two ways to interpret his words to Timothy. The New American Bible says that God will guard "what has been entrusted to me"—the gospel, the Christian faith. Other versions say that God will preserve "what I have entrusted to him," which could mean Paul's life, his work, or his converts. Both translations emphasize God's protection. God guards the faith, and God guards the faithful.

2 Timothy 1:1–3, 6–12
Psalm 123
Mark 12:18–27

Remind people of these things and charge them before God to stop disputing about words. This serves no useful purpose since it harms those who listen.

—2 TIMOTHY 2:14

At the heart of Paul's gospel was this belief: "If we have died with him / we shall also live with him; / if we persevere / we shall also reign with him" (2:11–12). What is at the heart of your faith? For the good of others, can you focus on that and let lesser things go?

2 Timothy 2:8–15
Psalm 25
Mark 12:28–34

All scripture is inspired by God and is useful for teaching, for refutation, for correction, and for training in righteousness, so that one who belongs to God may be competent, equipped for every good work.

—2 TIMOTHY 3:16–17

Scripture is a primary source of a Christian's beliefs about God. It is much more than a book of doctrine, however. It is also a guide for everyday life. It holds up high standards of justice and mercy, and it tells us when we go off the rails. Scripture study prepares us both intellectually and practically to do the work God gives us.

2 Timothy 3:10–17
Psalm 119
Mark 12:35–37

{B}e persistent whether it is convenient or inconvenient.

—2 TIMOTHY 4:2

It's easy to persist, even in a difficult project, when I'm well rested, enjoying myself, and unhurried. But what about when I have had only four or five hours of sleep . . . am bored silly . . . have more work than I can possibly do . . . know that sixteen other tasks are vying for my attention?

2 Timothy 4:1–8
Psalm 71
Mark 12:38–44

As Jesus passed on from there, he saw a man named Matthew sitting at the customs post. He said to him, "Follow me." And he got up and followed him. While he was at table in his house, many tax collectors and sinners came and sat with Jesus and his disciples. The Pharisees saw this and said to his disciples, "Why does your teacher eat with tax collectors and sinners?"

—MATTHEW 9:9–11

Some six hundred years before Christ, Aesop wrote: "A man is known by the company he keeps." Why did Jesus hang out with disreputable people?

Hosea 6:3–6
Psalm 50
Romans 4:18–25
Matthew 9:9–13

The LORD then said to Elijah. . . . "You shall drink of the stream, and I have commanded ravens to feed you there." . . . Ravens brought him bread and meat in the morning, and bread and meat in the evening, and he drank from the stream.

—1 KINGS 17:2, 4, 6

Famine doesn't worry ravens, because they love to eat dead and decaying animals. How kind of them to share their tasty morsels with Elijah! God provides, but he doesn't coddle.

1 Kings 17:1–6
Psalm 121
Matthew 5:1–12

After some time, however, the brook ran dry, because no rain had fallen in the land. So the LORD said to him: "Move on to Zarephath of Sidon and stay there. I have designated a widow there to provide for you."

—1 KINGS 17:7–9

Why would God send Elijah to a widow's house? Who was providing for her? No one, as it turned out. She and her child were down to their last meal. It took great faith for Elijah to ask her for a bite—and even greater faith for her to offer it.

1 Kings 17:7–16
Psalm 4
Matthew 5:13–16

{T}hey sent Barnabas [to go] to Antioch. When he arrived and saw the grace of God, he rejoiced and encouraged them all to remain faithful to the Lord in firmness of heart, for he was a good man, filled with the holy Spirit and faith.

—ACTS 11:22–24

Barnabas's name means "son of encouragement" (Acts 4:36), and Barnabas's nature was to appreciate and give thanks for the goodness he found in others. Do you have a Barnabas in your life? Are you a Barnabas to somebody else?

Acts 11:21b–26; 13:1–3
Psalm 98
Matthew 5:17–19

"Climb up and look out to sea," he directed his servant, who went up and looked, but reported, "There is nothing." Seven times he said, "Go, look again!" And the seventh time the youth reported, "There is a cloud as small as a man's hand rising from the sea." Elijah said, "Go and say to Ahab, 'Harness up and leave the mountain before the rain stops you.'"

—1 KINGS 18:43–44

The faith-filled person is not the one who prays most eloquently for rain, but the one who brings an umbrella to the prayer meeting.

1 Kings 18:41–46
Psalm 65
Matthew 5:20–26

There he came to a cave, where he took shelter. But the word of the LORD came to him, "Why are you here, Elijah?"

—1 KINGS 19:9

Elijah apparently understood God's question to mean "What has brought you to this point?" and he answered by describing the dangers he had faced. God, however, meant it a different way: "What have you been appointed to do?"

1 Kings 19:9a, 11–16
Psalm 27
Matthew 5:27–32

Elisha left him and, taking the yoke of oxen, slaughtered them; he used the plowing equipment for fuel to boil their flesh, and gave it to his people to eat. Then he left and followed Elijah as his attendant.

—1 KINGS 19:21

Whenever we add something to our lives, no matter how good it is, we necessarily subtract something else. A new baby means less sleep. Volunteering at the food pantry means less time at home. Retirement means fewer opportunities to interact with colleagues. We can't do everything, but we can do whatever God calls us to do.

1 Kings 19:19–21
Psalm 16
Matthew 5:33–37

At the sight of the crowds, his heart was moved with pity for them because they were troubled and abandoned, like sheep without a shepherd.

—MATTHEW 9:36

If ever we feel troubled and abandoned by those who are supposed to be our spiritual leaders, we can still have faith that Jesus, the Good Shepherd, is always available to help us.

Exodus 19:2–6a
Psalm 100
Romans 5:6–11
Matthew 9:36–10:8

Ahab said to Naboth, "Give me your vineyard to be my vegetable garden, since it is close by, next to my house." . . . "The LORD forbid," Naboth answered him, "that I should give you my ancestral heritage."

Ahab went home disturbed and angry at the answer Naboth the Jezreelite had made to him. . . . Lying down on his bed, he turned away from food and would not eat.

—1 KINGS 21:2–4

Coveting—wanting what belongs to someone else—seems so harmless. What's wrong with fantasizing about what you'd like to have? Why is "You shall not covet" part of the Ten Commandments (Exodus 20:17)? Read the whole appalling story about Ahab, Jezebel, and Naboth, and see where coveting can lead.

1 Kings 21:1–16
Psalm 5
Matthew 5:38–42

Indeed, no one gave himself up to the doing of evil in the sight of the LORD as did Ahab, urged on by his wife Jezebel. He became completely abominable by following idols, just as the Amorites had done, whom the LORD drove out before the Israelites.

—1 KINGS 21:25–26

Actions have consequences, and Ahab's wickedness would lead to the ruin of his dynasty. Amazingly, God had mercy even on the abominable Ahab: "Since he has humbled himself before me, I will not bring the evil in his time" (21:29). No one is beyond God's grace.

1 Kings 21:17–29
Psalm 51
Matthew 5:43–48

JUNE 18

*As they walked on conversing, a flaming chariot and flaming horses
came between them, and Elijah went up to heaven in a whirlwind.*

—2 KINGS 2:11

Over and over, the Bible tells of God's dramatic deliverance
of his people. American slaves sang about these biblical
rescues as they planned their own escapes. When they
heard someone humming "Swing Low, Sweet Chariot" in
the middle of the night, they knew it was more than a song
about Elijah. It was a signal to get on the Underground
Railroad and head for freedom.

2 Kings 2:1, 6–14
Psalm 31
Matthew 6:1–6, 16–18

Thursday

JUNE 19

• ST. ROMUALD, ABBOT •

How awesome are you, ELIJAH!
Whose glory is equal to yours? . . .
You were taken aloft in a whirlwind,
in a chariot with fiery horses.
You are destined, it is written, in time to come
to put an end to wrath before the day of the LORD.
—SIRACH 48:4, 9–10

Christians and Jews alike revere the prophet Elijah. Jewish tradition holds that Elijah will return to prepare the way for the Messiah. Christians believe that John the Baptist came "in the spirit and power of Elijah" (Luke 1:17) to prepare the way for Jesus.

Sirach 48:1–14
Psalm 97
Matthew 6:7–15

⋺ 203 ⋲

When Athaliah, the mother of Ahaziah, saw that her son was dead,
she began to kill off the whole royal family. But Jehosheba, . . . sister
of Ahaziah, took Joash, his son. . . . She concealed him from Athaliah,
and so he did not die.

—2 KINGS 11:1–2

Athaliah, weak Ahab's wicked daughter, almost fulfilled
Elijah's prophecy that Ahab's line would be destroyed
(1 Kings 21:21–24). She did not count on Jehosheba's act
of kindness, however. This good woman hid Athaliah's
baby grandson, who would become king and restore the
temple that his grandmother had damaged. Because of one
woman's compassion, King David's dynasty continued.

2 Kings 11:1–4, 9–18, 20
Psalm 132
Matthew 6:19–23

*After the death of Jehoiada, the princes of Judah came and paid homage
to the king, and the king then listened to them. They forsook the temple
of the LORD, the God of their fathers.*

—2 CHRONICLES 24:17–18

Joash was a good king for as long as his uncle Jehoiada
lived. Once the great old man died, however, the king
listened to the wrong advisers, and soon the whole
kingdom fell right back into idol worship. When
Zechariah, Jehoiada's son, protested, the king had him
killed. Then an enemy tribe trashed Joash's kingdom.
The king fell ill, and his own servants finished him off.
One moral of this story: if you depend on advisers,
pick them carefully!

2 Chronicles 24:17–25
Psalm 89
Matthew 6:24–34

And do not be afraid of those who kill the body but cannot kill the soul; rather, be afraid of the one who can destroy both soul and body in Gehenna.

—MATTHEW 10:28

Saints are people who can endure any hardship, bear any indignity, face any danger—even death—because they know their souls are safe.

Jeremiah 20:10–13
Psalm 69
Romans 5:12–15
Matthew 10:26–33

JUNE 23

And though the LORD warned Israel and Judah by every prophet and seer, "Give up your evil ways and keep my commandments and statutes, in accordance with the entire law which I enjoined on your fathers and which I sent you by my servants the prophets," they did not listen, but were as stiff-necked as their fathers, who had not believed in the LORD, their God.

—2 KINGS 17:13–14

How callously our society disregards human life, the environment, the needs of the poor! If only the Lord still spoke to the world through prophets . . . But would it make a difference? Have we ever listened?

2 Kings 17:5–8, 13–15a, 18
Psalm 60
Matthew 7:1–5

{T}hey were going to call him Zechariah after his father, but his mother
said in reply, "No. He will be called John." But they answered her,
"There is no one among your relatives who has this name." So they
made signs, asking his father what he wished him to be called. He asked
for a tablet and wrote, "John is his name," and all were amazed.

—LUKE 1:59–63

Israel was expecting a prophet to pave the way for the
Messiah, and the people had an idea of who that prophet
would be. Everything about John was unexpected—his
birth, his name, his lifestyle, his message, his death.
Sometimes our expectations keep us from seeing what's
really happening.

Vigil:	**Day:**
Jeremiah 1:4–10	Isaiah 49:1–6
Psalm 71	Psalm 139
1 Peter 1:8–12	Acts 13:22–26
Luke 1:5–17	Luke 1:57–66, 80

JUNE 25

The high priest Hilkiah informed the scribe Shaphan, "I have found the book of the law in the temple of the LORD." . . . The scribe Shaphan . . . then read it aloud to the king. When the king had heard the contents of the book of the law, he tore his garments.

—2 KINGS 22:8, 10–11

Josiah "conducted himself unswervingly just as his ancestor David had done" (22:2), but the only life he knew was bathed in evil. His grandfather, a man of legendary cruelty, had worshiped many gods, profaned the temple, and even sacrificed his son in a pagan ritual (see 21:1–18). When Josiah heard the law for the first time, he realized just how corrupt his kingdom had become. The law inspired him to launch a major reform that would restore monotheism to Judah.

2 Kings 22:8–13; 23:1–3
Psalm 119
Matthew 7:15–20

JUNE 26

Jehoiachin was eighteen years old when he began to reign, and he reigned three months in Jerusalem. . . . He did evil in the sight of the LORD, just as his forebears had done.

At that time the officials of Nebuchadnezzar, king of Babylon, attacked Jerusalem, and the city came under siege.

—2 KINGS 24:8–10

Though Jehoiachin was as bad as his predecessors, the invasion of Jerusalem wasn't the fault of this teenager who had been king for only a few weeks. For more than three hundred years, Judah had been growing ever more corrupt. Left alone, it would surely have destroyed itself. But stripped of their possessions and uprooted to a new land, the people just might be shocked into turning back to God.

2 Kings 24:8–17
Psalm 79
Matthew 7:21–29

He burned the house of the LORD, the palace of the king, and all the houses of Jerusalem; every large building was destroyed by fire.

—2 KINGS 25:9

The destruction was total. Fire swept away their Vatican, their Washington, DC, their workplaces, their shopping malls, their homes. Then Babylonian troops led all but the poorest among them into exile. What was left of their former lives? Only the continuing love of a God they barely knew.

2 Kings 25:1–12
Psalm 137
Matthew 8:1–4

JUNE 28

Your prophets had for you
false and specious visions;
They did not lay bare your guilt,
to avert your fate;
They beheld for you in vision
false and misleading portents.

—LAMENTATIONS 2:14

The prescribing instructions for some medications warn of a dangerous side effect: a "false sense of well-being."

Lamentations 2:2, 10–14, 18–19
Psalm 74
Matthew 8:5–17

Then Peter . . . said, "Now I know for certain that [the] Lord sent his angel and rescued me from the hand of Herod."

—ACTS 12:11

The Lord will rescue me from every evil threat and will bring me safe to his heavenly kingdom.

—2 TIMOTHY 4:18

Time after time, God rescued Peter and Paul from danger. Yet eventually Peter was crucified and Paul was beheaded. Why didn't God rescue them from martyrdom? What does it mean to be brought "safe to his heavenly kingdom"?

Vigil:	**Day:**
Acts 3:1–10	Acts 12:1–11
Psalm 19	Psalm 34
Galatians 1:11–20	2 Timothy 4:6–8, 17–18
John 21:15–19	Matthew 16:13–19

Thus says the LORD:
For three crimes of Israel, and for four,
I will not revoke my word;
Because they sell the just man for silver,
and the poor man for a pair of sandals.

—AMOS 2:6

Nowadays the horrors of slavery are obvious. But Western consumerism continues to create conditions that lead to exploitation and even enslavement in the "two-thirds world." What is the human cost of diamonds and handmade rugs, inexpensive clothing and cheap bananas? Are we willing to spend more in order to promote fair trade?

Amos 2:6–10, 13–16
Psalm 50
Matthew 8:18–22

⇒ 214 ⇐

I brought upon you such upheaval
as when God overthrew Sodom and Gomorrah: . . .
Yet you returned not to me,
says the LORD.

—AMOS 4:11

Do hard times make people turn to God? Not necessarily,
says the prophet Amos. Then do God's rich blessings draw
people to him? Another prophet notes, "{W}hen filled, they
became proud of heart / and forgot me" (Hosea 13:6). And
yet in good times and bad, some people do respond to
God. If not the circumstances of our lives, what is it that
nudges us to grow in faith?

Amos 3:1–8; 4:11–12
Psalm 5
Matthew 8:23–27

Away with your noisy songs!
I will not listen to the melodies of your harps. . . .
let justice surge like water,
and goodness like an unfailing stream.

—A MOS 5 : 2 3 – 2 4

It's not that God dislikes music: "Come before him with joyful song," wrote the psalmist (Psalm 100:2). It's just that piety can never replace right action. Going to church on Sunday does not excuse us from behaving ethically on Wednesday.

Amos 5:14–15, 21–24
Psalm 50
Matthew 8:28–34

Thursday

JULY 3

• ST. THOMAS, APOSTLE •

*But {Thomas} said to {the other disciples}, "Unless I see the mark of
the nails in his hands and put my finger into the nailmarks and put my
hand into his side, I will not believe."*

—JOHN 20:25

Some saints believe easily; some, like Thomas, require
evidence. Scripture does not demand gullible belief. It
encourages us to ask questions, to put our beliefs to the
test. "{D}o not trust every spirit," wrote an early Christian
leader, "but test the spirits to see whether they belong to
God, because many false prophets have gone out into the
world" (1 John 4:1). Doubt can help us arrive at truth.

Ephesians 2:19–22
Psalm 117
John 20:24–29

Friday

JULY 4

• ST. ELIZABETH OF PORTUGAL • INDEPENDENCE DAY •

*Hear this, you who trample upon the needy
and destroy the poor of the land! . . .*

*I will turn your feasts into mourning
and all your songs into lamentations.*

—AMOS 8:4, 10

Do we guarantee life, liberty, and the pursuit of happiness
to all Americans, or only to the strong? Do we share our
material blessings so that all people have adequate food,
clothing, and shelter?

"O say, does that star-spangled banner yet wave
O'er the land of the free and the home of the brave?"

Amos 8:4–6, 9–12
Psalm 119
Matthew 9:9–13

Saturday

JULY 5

• ST. ANTHONY MARY ZACCARIA, PRIEST •

I will bring about the restoration of my people Israel;
they shall rebuild and inhabit their ruined cities,
Plant vineyards and drink the wine,
set out gardens and eat the fruits.
I will plant them upon their own ground;
never again shall they be plucked
From the land I have given them,
say I, the LORD, your God.

—AMOS 9:14–15

This is true wealth—a home and a community, plentiful food and drink, divine protection. When the whole world enjoys these blessings, God's restoration will be complete.

Amos 9:11–15
Psalm 85
Matthew 9:14–17

*Come to me, all you who labor and are burdened,
and I will give you rest.*

—MATTHEW 11:28

Medication, exercise, meditation, a healthy diet, rest,
vitamins, vacations, Sabbath keeping—any of these can
help relieve stress, and some are absolutely necessary.
These fine stress busters, however, are even more
effective in a person who has faith in God's goodness
and Jesus' love.

Zechariah 9:9–10
Psalm 145
Romans 8:9, 11–13
Matthew 11:25–30

I will espouse you to me forever:
I will espouse you in right and in justice,
in love and in mercy.
—HOSEA 2:21

The parishioners were in disagreement. One side based its judgment on law: "We know what is right, and this behavior is clearly wrong, and we can't in good conscience accept it, even though we love the people who do these things." The other side based its judgment on love: "We love these people, and they love each other, so their behavior can't be wrong, even though it goes against church teaching." How can we, like God, bring justice and mercy together?

Hosea 2:16, 17b–18, 21–22
Psalm 145
Matthew 9:18–26

The work of an artisan,
no god at all,
Destined for the flames—
such is the calf of Samaria!

—HOSEA 8:6

A king of Israel had built calf idols for God's people to worship, and the prophet Hosea was pointing out the obvious: man-made, destructible things are no gods at all. Calf idols aren't big in my midwestern suburb, but a whole lot of us put inordinate trust in our net worth.

Hosea 8:4–7, 11–13
Psalm 115
Matthew 9:32–38

Sow for yourselves justice,
reap the fruit of piety;
Break up for yourselves a new field,
for it is time to seek the LORD,
till he come and rain down justice upon you.

—HOSEA 10:12

Sometimes we get it backward—we sow piety, hoping to
reap justice. That is, we think that if we pray enough about
the poor, the oppressed, and the persecuted, God will take
care of them for us. Hosea advises us to work for justice,
and then our prayers will be abundantly answered.

Hosea 10:1–3, 7–8, 12
Psalm 105
Matthew 10:1–7

When Israel was a child I loved him. . . .
{It} was I who taught Ephraim to walk,
who took them in my arms; . . .
I fostered them like one
who raises an infant to his cheeks;
Yet, though I stooped to feed my child,
they did not know that I was their healer.

—HOSEA 11:1, 3–4

Read this beautiful poem aloud and feel the tender love of God our Father. Personalize it by saying your own name or the name of your parish instead of "Israel" and "Ephraim." Thank the Father for nurturing and healing you.

Hosea 11:1–4, 8c–9
Psalm 80
Matthew 10:7–15

I will be like the dew for Israel:
he shall blossom like the lily;
He shall strike root like the Lebanon cedar,
and put forth his shoots.
His splendor shall be like the olive tree
and his fragrance like the Lebanon cedar.

—HOSEA 14:6–7

Hosea has been warning that Israel will be punished
severely, and yet healing and renewal will follow. The
motto of St. Benedict's abbey at Monte Cassino evokes
such a cycle of loss and restoration: *Succisa virescit,* "Pruned,
it grows again."

Hosea 14:2–10
Psalm 51
Matthew 10:16–23

"Holy, holy, holy is the LORD of hosts!" they cried one to the other. "All the earth is filled with his glory!" At the sound of that cry, the frame of the door shook and the house was filled with smoke.

Then I said, "Woe is me, I am doomed!" For I am a man of unclean lips, living among a people of unclean lips; yet my eyes have seen the King, the LORD of hosts!"

—ISAIAH 6:3–5

Does God exist in order to comfort us, to save us from predicaments, and to occasionally find us parking spaces? The prophet Isaiah didn't think so.

Isaiah 6:1–8
Psalm 93
Matthew 10:24–33

*The seed sown among thorns is the one who hears the word,
but then worldly anxiety and the lure of riches choke the word and
it bears no fruit.*

—MATTHEW 13:22

Worrying about making a living . . . Seeking the path to
success and riches . . . Searching for the last best thing to
buy and own . . . We humans have been doing these things
for millennia. The result? Stress. Fatigue. Meaninglessness.
Is there a better way to live?

Isaiah 55:10–11
Psalm 65
Romans 8:18–23
Matthew 13:1–23 or 13:1–9

Monday

JULY 14

• BD. KATERI TEKAKWITHA, VIRGIN •

Your new moons and festivals I detest;
they weigh me down, I tire of the load.
When you spread out your hands,
I close my eyes to you;
Though you pray the more,
I will not listen.
Your hands are full of blood!
—ISAIAH 1:14–15

"As part of the spiritual worship acceptable to God . . . ,
the Gospel of life is to be celebrated above all in daily
living, which should be filled with self-giving love for
others. In this way, our lives will become a genuine and
responsible acceptance of the gift of life and a heartfelt
song of praise and gratitude to God who has given us this
gift" (Pope John Paul II).

Isaiah 1:10–17
Psalm 50
Matthew 10:34–11:1

Tuesday

JULY 15

• ST. BONAVENTURE, BISHOP AND DOCTOR OF THE CHURCH •

*Unless your faith is firm
you shall not be firm!*
—ISAIAH 7:9

When Franklin D. Roosevelt came into office in 1933,
America was in the midst of the Great Depression. The
opening words of his inaugural address echo Isaiah's advice
to King Ahaz: "This great Nation will endure as it has
endured, will revive and will prosper. So, first of all, let me
assert my firm belief that the only thing we have to fear is
fear itself—nameless, unreasoning, unjustified terror which
paralyzes needed efforts to convert retreat into advance."

Isaiah 7:1–9
Psalm 48
Matthew 11:20–24

Wednesday

JULY 16

"By my own power I have done it,
and by my wisdom, for I am shrewd." . . .
Will the axe boast against him who hews with it?
Will the saw exalt itself above him who wields it?
—ISAIAH 10:13, 15

Who deserves the credit for our accomplishments?

Isaiah 10:5–7, 13b–16
Psalm 94
Matthew 11:25–27

Salvation we have not achieved for the earth,
the inhabitants of the world cannot bring it forth.
But your dead shall live, their corpses shall rise;
awake and sing, you who lie in the dust.

—ISAIAH 26:18–19

Even though we cannot bring peace among nations or heal
the wounded environment or teach all humans to love,
we must keep working toward those goals. Even though
our imperfect work will soon be forgotten, God will one
day bring salvation, restoration, and resurrection to all the
inhabitants of the world.

Isaiah 26:7–9, 12, 16–19
Psalm 102
Matthew 11:28–30

In those days, when Hezekiah was mortally ill, the prophet Isaiah . . .
came and said to him: "Thus says the LORD: *Put your house in order,*
for you are about to die; you shall not recover."

—ISAIAH 38:1

If the Lord sent a prophet to your door with a message like
this, what would you do?

Isaiah 38:1–6, 21–22, 7–8
Isaiah 38:10–12, 16
Matthew 12:1–8

Woe to those who plan iniquity. . . .
In the morning light they accomplish it
when it lies within their power.
They covet fields, and seize them;
houses, and they take them;
They cheat an owner of his house,
a man of his inheritance.

—MICAH 2:1–2

Suppose your company wanted to do something that
is perfectly legal, would increase your company's profit
margin, would allow for expansion, and might even
result in a nice raise for you—but would mean laying off
employees. Would it be a moral thing to do? Would you
think it was moral if you were one of the laid-off workers?

Micah 2:1–5
Psalm 10
Matthew 12:14–21

{I}f you pull up the weeds you might uproot the wheat along with them. Let them grow together until harvest; then at harvest time I will say to the harvesters, "First collect the weeds and tie them in bundles for burning; but gather the wheat into my barn."

—MATTHEW 13:29–30

"Stop judging," Jesus said to his disciples (Matthew 7:1), but he didn't say there would be no judgment. Between now and Judgment Day, though, we don't have enough information, enough love, or enough understanding of God's purposes to know who is in God's kingdom and who is not.

Wisdom 12:13, 16–19
Psalm 86
Romans 8:26–27
Matthew 13:24–43 or 13:24–30

He has showed you, O man, what is good;
and what does the Lord require of you
but to do justice, and to love kindness,
and to walk humbly with your God?
—MICAH 6:8 (RSV)

This one little verse tells us all we need to know about living with integrity. Read it aloud: it sings. Instead of "O man," say your name. Memorize the verse and repeat it every day as a reminder of what is truly important.

Micah 6:1–4, 6–8
Psalm 50
Matthew 12:38–42

Tuesday

JULY 22

• ST. MARY MAGDALENE •

But Mary stayed outside the tomb weeping.

—JOHN 20:11

When we experience grief, we may try to keep pain at bay by denying our feelings, working ourselves to the point of exhaustion, or medicating ourselves into numbness. Mary chose a better way: she stayed with her pain, allowing its full force to wash over her. And that is why she saw the angels, and spoke with the man she thought was the gardener, and then found herself face-to-face with Jesus.

Micah 7:14–15, 18–20
Psalm 63
John 20:1–2, 11–18

"Ah, Lord GOD!" I said,
"I know not how to speak; I am too young."

—JEREMIAH 1:6

How much good has been done by supposedly unqualified people! Mother Teresa was a foreign Christian woman in a male-dominated, largely Hindu country. Abraham Lincoln was born in a log cabin to illiterate farmers. The Blessed Virgin Mary was an unmarried teenager from a town with a bad reputation. If God called only well-qualified people, a lot of important things wouldn't get done.

Jeremiah 1:1, 4–10
Psalm 71
Matthew 13:1–9

⇒ 237 ⇐

Two evils have my people done:
they have forsaken me, the source of living waters;
They have dug themselves cisterns,
broken cisterns, that hold no water.

—JEREMIAH 2:13

Why try to replace God's gracious gifts with things we do
for ourselves? Are we afraid of losing control?

Jeremiah 2:1–3, 7–8, 12–13
Psalm 36
Matthew 13:10–17

He said to her, "What do you wish?" She answered him, "Command that these two sons of mine sit, one at your right and the other at your left, in your kingdom." Jesus said in reply, "You do not know what you are asking. Can you drink the cup that I am going to drink?" They said to him, "We can."

—MATTHEW 20:21–22

Poor deluded James and John. With Peter, they were Jesus' favorite disciples, yet they didn't understand him at all. They thought that being close to Jesus would mean health, prosperity, and power. Instead, it meant persecution, exile, and martyrdom.

2 Corinthians 4:7–15
Psalm 126
Matthew 20:20–28

Are you to steal and murder, commit adultery and perjury, burn incense to Baal, go after strange gods that you know not, and yet come to stand before me in this house which bears my name, and say: "We are safe; we can commit all these abominations again"?

—JEREMIAH 7:9–10

"The movement of return to God, called conversion and repentance, entails sorrow for and abhorrence of sins committed, and the firm purpose of sinning no more in the future. Conversion touches the past and the future and is nourished by hope in God's mercy" (*Catechism of the Catholic Church*, 1490).

Jeremiah 7:1–11
Psalm 84
Matthew 13:24–30

The kingdom of heaven is like a treasure buried in a field, which a person finds and hides again, and out of joy goes and sells all that he has and buys that field.

—MATTHEW 13:44

When we think of all we must do and all we must give up to attain the kingdom of heaven, it can sound grim indeed. But this parable puts a different spin on it: the kingdom of heaven is a treasure that inspires joy. To get that treasure and feel that joy, we give up everything we previously valued—not out of duty, but because nothing can compare with the kingdom's richness.

1 Kings 3:5, 7–12
Psalm 119
Romans 8:28–30
Matthew 13:44–52 or 13:44–46

For, as close as the loincloth clings to a man's loins, so had I made the whole house of Israel and the whole house of Judah cling to me, says the LORD; to be my people, my renown, my praise, my beauty. But they did not listen.

—JEREMIAH 13:11

What can be more painful than unrequited love . . . and who can grieve more deeply than God?

Jeremiah 13:1–11
Deuteronomy 32:18–21
Matthew 13:31–35

Martha, burdened with much serving, came to him and said, "Lord, do you not care that my sister has left me by myself to do the serving? Tell her to help me."

—LUKE 10:40

Actually, Jesus cared a lot about Martha. He didn't want her slaving away in the kitchen all by herself. But his solution to her problem was not the one she expected. Cut back the menu, he suggested, and come join the guests. Jesus doesn't always solve our problems in the way we expect—thank God!

Jeremiah 14:17–22
Psalm 79
John 11:19–27 or Luke 10:38–42

JULY 30

• ST. PETER CHRYSOLOGUS, BISHOP AND DOCTOR OF THE CHURCH •

Why is my pain continuous,
my wound incurable, refusing to be healed?
—JEREMIAH 15:18

Often called the "weeping prophet," Jeremiah had a
sensitive nature. He deeply felt God's frustration with his
people. At the same time, he loved his people, and he was
wounded when they rejected God's overtures. Jeremiah's
passion for both God and God's people caused him
great personal suffering, yet it uniquely equipped him to
understand and portray God's self-sacrificing love.

Jeremiah 15:10, 16–21
Psalm 59
Matthew 13:44–46

I went down to the potter's house and there he was, working at the wheel. Whenever the object of clay which he was making turned out badly in his hand, he tried again, making of the clay another object of whatever sort he pleased.

—JEREMIAH 18:3–4

God adapts his plans to our response. If we mess up plan A, he introduces plan B. If we stop fighting him and start cooperating, he goes back to plan A. God may use suffering as a tool, but his constant goal is to restore a loving relationship between himself and humanity.

Jeremiah 18:1–6
Psalm 146
Matthew 13:47–53

When Jeremiah finished speaking all that the LORD bade him speak to all the people, the priests and prophets laid hold of him, crying, "You must be put to death!"

—JEREMIAH 26:8

Jeremiah warned the people that if they did not change their ways, their nation would be in big trouble. His words were true, but truth hurts. Do we vote for politicians who warn that we must radically cut back on oil consumption, or who insist on raising taxes to cover necessary social programs? Do we like preachers who point out that our sexual behavior is destroying our society, or who suggest that we need to confess and forsake our sins?

Jeremiah 26:1–9
Psalm 69
Matthew 13:54–58

Now, therefore, reform your ways and your deeds; listen to the voice of the LORD your God, so that the LORD will repent of the evil with which he threatens you.

—JEREMIAH 26:13

Does God lay hidden traps so he can zap us if we stumble and fall into them? Or does God warn us of pitfalls ahead so we can avoid them and keep on walking with him?

Jeremiah 26:11–16, 24
Psalm 69
Matthew 14:1–12

[Jesus] said to them, "There is no need for them to go away; give them some food yourselves." But they said to him, "Five loaves and two fish are all we have here." Then he said, "Bring them here to me."

—MATTHEW 14:16–18

The world's needs are vast and growing. The church's resources cannot possibly keep up—unless we bring what we have to Jesus.

Isaiah 55:1–3
Psalm 145
Romans 8:35, 37–39
Matthew 14:13–21

*To the prophet Hananiah the prophet Jeremiah said: Hear this,
Hananiah! The LORD has not sent you, and you have raised false
confidence in this people.*

—JEREMIAH 28:15

Would you rather listen to a speaker who gives you
confidence, makes you feel good, and motivates you to go
out and do your best—or to a speaker who is completely
honest with you, even when the truth hurts?

Jeremiah 28:1–17
Psalm 119
Matthew 14:22–36

AUGUST 5

You shall be my people,
and I will be your God.
—JEREMIAH 30:22

This is the covenant God made with Abraham (Genesis 17:8), repeated at the time of the escape from Egypt (Exodus 6:7), and renewed through the prophets and the New Testament writers. The promise applies to God's people as a community and also as individuals. In the book of Revelation, God says: "The victor will inherit these gifts, and I shall be his God, and he will be my son" (21:7). The Lord of heaven and earth is our God, and we are his much-loved sons and daughters.

Jeremiah 30:1–2, 12–15, 18–22
Psalm 102
Matthew 14:22–36 or 15:1–2, 10–14

We ourselves heard this voice come from heaven while we were with him
on the holy mountain.

—2 PETER 1:18

Scripture is not a collection of "cleverly devised myths" (1:16), nor is it a legal code, a handbook for living, a theological system, or a crystal ball. It is rather the story of God reaching out to human beings, and human beings experiencing God's presence. Peter, James, and John were eyewitnesses to Jesus' transfiguration (Matthew 17:1–8). They heard the voice from heaven. They knew that Jesus was God's Son.

Daniel 7:9–10, 13–14
Psalm 97
2 Peter 1:16–19
Matthew 17:1–9

AUGUST 7

The days are coming, says the LORD, when I will make a new covenant with the house of Israel and the house of Judah. . . . I will place my law within them, and write it upon their hearts; I will be their God, and they shall be my people.

—JEREMIAH 31:31, 33

When we see as God sees,
hear as God hears,
feel as God feels,
and love as God loves,
then we will do as God does.

Jeremiah 31:31–34
Psalm 51
Matthew 16:13–23

AUGUST 8

• ST. DOMINIC, PRIEST •

Woe to the bloody city, all lies,
full of plunder, whose looting never stops!
The crack of the whip, the rumbling sounds of wheels;
horses a-gallop, chariots bounding,
Cavalry charging,
The flame of the sword, the flash of the spear,
the many slain, the heaping corpses,
the endless bodies to stumble upon!

—NAHUM 3:1–3

It has been twenty-six hundred years since Nahum described the horrors of war. In all that time, what have we learned?

Nahum 2:1, 3; 3:1–3, 6–7
Deuteronomy 32:35–36, 39, 41
Matthew 16:24–28

AUGUST 9

• ST. TERESA BENEDICTA OF THE CROSS, VIRGIN AND MARTYR •

Too pure are your eyes to look upon evil,
and the sight of misery you cannot endure.
Why, then, do you gaze on the faithless in silence
while the wicked man devours
one more just than himself?

—HABAKKUK 1:13

God is good. God hates suffering. Then why do bad things happen to good people? Habakkuk does not answer this age-old philosophical question. He does, however, express confidence that God will "come forth to save {God's} people" (3:13), and he vows he will "rejoice in the LORD" no matter what happens in the meantime (3:17–18).

Habakkuk 1:12–2:4
Psalm 9
Matthew 17:14–20

AUGUST 10

Peter got out of the boat and began to walk on the water toward Jesus. But when he saw how [strong] the wind was he became frightened; and, beginning to sink, he cried out, "Lord, save me!" Immediately Jesus stretched out his hand and caught him, and said to him, "O you of little faith, why did you doubt?"

—MATTHEW 14:29–31

I'm pretty impressed with Peter's faith, actually. After all, he did get out of that boat and start to walk on water, which is a lot more than the other disciples did. Maybe the problem began when Peter got too impressed with his own faith. Maybe, just for a moment, he thought he was walking on water by his own power.

1 Kings 19:9a, 11–13a
Psalm 85
Romans 9:1–5
Matthew 14:22–33

*On the fifth day of the month, the fifth year, that is, of King
Jehoiachin's exile, the word of the LORD came to the priest Ezekiel . . . in
the land of the Chaldeans by the river Chebar.*

—EZEKIEL 1:2–3

The great Babylonian Empire had conquered Judah.
Ezekiel, along with many other Jews, was now a captive
and an exile. The good news: God followed his people
into Babylon and continued sending messages through
prophets. The bad news: Jerusalem would soon be
destroyed. The best news: destruction is never God's last
word. Stay tuned.

Ezekiel 1:2–5, 24–28c
Psalm 148
Matthew 17:22–27

Son of man, he then said to me, feed your belly and fill your stomach with this scroll I am giving you. I ate it, and it was as sweet as honey in my mouth. He said: Son of man, go now to the house of Israel, and speak my words to them.

—EZEKIEL 3:3–4

Mystics speak of "consolations," the passionate, sensual spirituality sometimes experienced as people first become aware of God's presence. The spiritual honeymoon, though lovely, is fleeting. Later, when Ezekiel's mission would drive him to grief and exhaustion, would he draw strength from a remembered taste of honey?

Ezekiel 2:8–3:4
Psalm 119
Matthew 18:1–5, 10, 12–14

Old men, youths and maidens, women and children—wipe them out!
But do not touch any marked with the X.

—EZEKIEL 9:6

Exodus 12 tells a similar story. On the night when Israel
escaped from slavery, the Lord killed the firstborn of
Egypt but spared the people of Israel who had marked
their doorposts with the blood of a lamb. Do these stories
describe God's judgment of evil, or God's mercy toward
his people? Is it possible to separate mercy from judgment?

Ezekiel 9:1–7; 10:18–22
Psalm 113
Matthew 18:15–20

Son of man, you live in the midst of a rebellious house; they have eyes to see but do not see, and ears to hear but do not hear, for they are a rebellious house. Now, son of man, during the day while they are looking on, prepare your baggage as though for exile, and again while they are looking on, migrate from where you live to another place; perhaps they will see that they are a rebellious house.

—EZEKIEL 12:2–3

No one was paying any attention to what the prophets were saying, so God told Ezekiel to find an audience and stage a one-man play. God does whatever it takes to get our attention.

Ezekiel 12:1–12
Psalm 78
Matthew 18:21–19:1

⇒ 259 ⇐

But now Christ has been raised from the dead, the firstfruits of those
who have fallen asleep. For since death came through a human being,
the resurrection of the dead came also through a human being. For just
as in Adam all die, so too in Christ shall all be brought to life.

—1 CORINTHIANS 15:20–22

As a daughter of Adam, Mary died. As a person saved by
God's grace, Mary was raised from the dead, given her
resurrection body (15:36–44), and welcomed into heaven.
As the mother of the church, she shows what lies in store
for those who put their faith in Christ.

Vigil:	**Day:**
1 Chronicles 15:3–4, 15–16; 16:1–2	Revelation 11:19a; 12:1–6a, 10ab
Psalm 132	Psalm 45
1 Corinthians 15:54b–57	1 Corinthians 15:20–27
Luke 11:27–28	Luke 1:39–56

Cast away from you all the crimes you have committed, and make for yourselves a new heart and a new spirit. Why should you die, O house of Israel? For I have no pleasure in the death of anyone who dies, says the Lord GOD. Return and live!

—EZEKIEL 18:31–32

You may have heard some pretty bad things about God— that he's vicious toward his enemies (especially in the Old Testament), for example, or that Jesus died to keep God from zapping the rest of us. Not true. As the prophets repeatedly proclaimed, God's aim is to give life and joy, peace and prosperity. God is always ready to forgive. Why don't we do our part?

Ezekiel 18:1–10, 13b, 30–32
Psalm 51
Matthew 19:13–15

AUGUST 17

Then Jesus said to her in reply, "O woman, great is your faith!
Let it be done for you as you wish." And her daughter was healed
from that hour.

—MATTHEW 15:28

Everything was stacked against her. She, a Gentile woman,
was asking Jesus, a Jewish man, to heal a child who was a
female and a Canaanite. But somehow this woman knew
that Jesus, unlike most of his contemporaries, valued
children as highly as adults, females as highly as males,
Canaanites as highly as Israelites.

Isaiah 56:1, 6–7
Psalm 67
Romans 11:13–15, 29–32
Matthew 15:21–28

AUGUST 18

• ST. JANE FRANCES DE CHANTAL, RELIGIOUS •

Thus says the Lord GOD: *I will now desecrate my sanctuary,
the stronghold of your pride, the delight of your eyes, the desire
of your soul.*

—EZEKIEL 24:21

What a grievous message—not only to the people who
heard it, but also to Ezekiel, who delivered it, and to God,
who spoke it. But what good was the temple when the
people were worshiping false gods?

Ezekiel 24:15–24
Deuteronomy 32:18–21
Matthew 19:16–22

By your great wisdom applied to your trading
you have heaped up your riches;
your heart has grown haughty from your riches—
therefore thus says the Lord GOD: . . .
I will bring against you
foreigners, the most barbarous of nations.

—EZEKIEL 28:5–7

Has any nation ever been attacked because it was too humble?

Ezekiel 28:1–10
Deuteronomy 32:26–28, 30, 35–36
Matthew 19:23–30

Thus says the Lord GOD: I swear I am coming against these shepherds.
I will claim my sheep from them and put a stop to their shepherding my
sheep so that they may no longer pasture themselves. I will save my
sheep, that they may no longer be food for their mouths.

—EZEKIEL 34:10

The shepherds—political and religious leaders—had
been using their position to fleece the people. Living
comfortably themselves, they had not provided adequate
food, health care, or protection for the people they led
(34:3–6). God's first concern, he told Ezekiel, was for the
sheep. The shepherds were dispensable.

Ezekiel 34:1–11
Psalm 23
Matthew 20:1–16

Thursday

AUGUST 21

• ST. PIUS X, POPE •

I will sprinkle clean water upon you to cleanse you from all your impurities, and from all your idols I will cleanse you. I will give you a new heart and place a new spirit within you, taking from your bodies your stony hearts and giving you natural hearts. I will put my spirit within you and make you live by my statutes, careful to observe my decrees.

—EZEKIEL 36:25–27

No question about it—God's people are often a sorry lot. And yet God's plan is to intervene and renew us, to give us a new heart and a new spirit and a new way of life.

Ezekiel 36:23–28
Psalm 51
Matthew 22:1–14

Then he said to me: Prophesy over these bones, and say to them: Dry bones, hear the word of the LORD!

—EZEKIEL 37:4

In Ezekiel's vision, Israel was a field of dry bones. But at God's word, those bones came together . . . grew flesh . . . were covered with skin . . . and began to breathe! Are we ever beyond God's power to restore?

Ezekiel 37:1–14
Psalm 107
Matthew 22:34–40

I saw that the temple was filled with the glory of the LORD. . . . The voice said to me: Son of man, this is where my throne shall be . . . ; here I will dwell among the Israelites forever.

—EZEKIEL 43:5, 7

It can't be said too often. All holy Scripture points to this one glorious reality: God is with us, and God will be with us forever.

Ezekiel 43:1–7ab
Psalm 85
Matthew 23:1–12

*{H}e asked his disciples, "Who do people say that the Son of Man is?"
They replied, "Some say John the Baptist, others Elijah, still others
Jeremiah or one of the prophets." He said to them, "But who do you say
that I am?"*

—MATTHEW 16:13–15

Picture Jesus sitting at your kitchen table with you and a
few of your friends. Suddenly Jesus looks directly at you
and says, "Who do you think I am? What do I mean to
you?" How do you respond?

Isaiah 22:19–23
Psalm 138
Romans 11:33–36
Matthew 16:13–20

We ought to thank God always for you, brothers, as is fitting, because your faith flourishes ever more, and the love of every one of you for one another grows ever greater.

—2 THESSALONIANS 1:3

According to Tertullian, a North African priest in the late second century, people were noticing something unusual about their Christian neighbors: "'See,' they say, 'how they love one another.'"

2 Thessalonians 1:1–5, 11–12
Psalm 96
Matthew 23:13–22

We ask you, brothers, with regard to the coming of our Lord Jesus Christ and our assembling with him, not to be shaken out of your minds suddenly, or to be alarmed either by a "spirit," or by an oral statement, or by a letter allegedly from us to the effect that the day of the Lord is at hand. Let no one deceive you in any way.

—2 THESSALONIANS 2:1–3

A few minutes on the Internet can yield hundreds of predictions of when the world will end. Most of them are already history. But, really, what does the date matter? Can't we trust Jesus to return when the time is right?

2 Thessalonians 2:1–3a, 14–17
Psalm 96
Matthew 23:23–26

{I}n toil and drudgery, night and day we worked, so as not to burden
any of you.

—2 THESSALONIANS 3:8

You can tell a lot about an organization by following
the money. Does most of it go to support the leaders'
affluent lifestyle? Or is as much as possible dedicated
to helping others?

2 Thessalonians 3:6–10, 16–18
Psalm 128
Matthew 23:27–32

⇒ 272 ⇐

He will keep you firm to the end, irreproachable on the day of our Lord Jesus [Christ]. God is faithful, and by him you were called to fellowship with his Son, Jesus Christ our Lord.

—1 CORINTHIANS 1:8–9

Sometimes the task is hard and the road is long. It's encouraging to know that if God has called me to it, God will keep me on it.

1 Corinthians 1:1–9
Psalm 145
Matthew 24:42–51

Friday

AUGUST 29

• THE MARTYRDOM OF ST. JOHN THE BAPTIST •

The girl hurried back to the king's presence and made her request, "I want you to give me at once on a platter the head of John the Baptist." The king was deeply distressed, but because of his oaths and the guests he did not wish to break his word to her.

—MARK 6:25–26

Because Herod was afraid of losing face, John lost his head.

1 Corinthians 1:17–25
Psalm 71
Mark 6:17–29

Not many of you were wise by human standards, not many were powerful, not many were of noble birth. Rather, God chose the foolish of the world to shame the wise, and God chose the weak of the world to shame the strong, and God chose the lowly and despised of the world, those who count for nothing, to reduce to nothing those who are something, so that no human being might boast before God.

—1 CORINTHIANS 1:26–29

Be honest with yourself: do these verses encourage you, or do they make you uneasy? If you realize they aren't talking about you, let them remind you to be more respectful of those who are less educated, less powerful, and less affluent than you are.

1 Corinthians 1:26–31
Psalm 33
Matthew 25:14–30

*From that time on, Jesus began to show his disciples that he must go
to Jerusalem and suffer greatly. . . . Then Peter took him aside and
began to rebuke him, "God forbid, Lord! No such thing shall ever
happen to you."*

—MATTHEW 16:21–22

When you are facing hard times, what do you want to hear
from your friends: "Don't worry—everything's going to be
OK" or "No matter what happens, I'm here for you"?

Jeremiah 20:7–9
Psalm 63
Romans 12:1–2
Matthew 16:21–27

{H}e has anointed me
to bring glad tidings to the poor.
He has sent me to proclaim liberty to captives
and recovery of sight to the blind,
to let the oppressed go free,
and to proclaim a year acceptable to the Lord.
—LUKE 4:18–19

The national election is approaching, and on this holiday
we'll hear plenty of political speeches. As we consider
which candidates to support, we need to ask: How will
their platforms and proposals affect the jobless, the
working poor, those who can't afford adequate health care?

1 Corinthians 2:1–5
Psalm 119
Luke 4:16–30

Now the natural person does not accept what pertains to the Spirit of God, for to him it is foolishness, and he cannot understand it, because it is judged spiritually.

—1 CORINTHIANS 2:14

Love your enemies. Go the second mile. Don't try to control people; serve them instead. Let others get the credit. Turn the other cheek. Don't worry about where your next meal is coming from. Give your wealth to the poor.

This is not normal behavior—but imagine a world where everyone acted like this.

1 Corinthians 2:10b–16
Psalm 145
Luke 4:31–37

*While there is jealousy and rivalry among you, are you not . . .
behaving in an ordinary human way? Whenever someone says,
"I belong to Paul," and another, "I belong to Apollos," are you not
merely human?*

—1 CORINTHIANS 3:3–4

"I'm only human," we say, excusing our bad behavior. Of
course we're jealous of people who get what we deserve.
Of course we compete for the top spots. Of course we
identify ourselves as conservatives or traditionalists or
liberals or progressives and feel superior to people in other
categories. We're only human, and we pay far too little
attention to the Spirit of God within us.

1 Corinthians 3:1–9
Psalm 33
Luke 4:38–44

Let no one deceive himself. If anyone among you considers himself wise in this age, let him become a fool so as to become wise.

—1 CORINTHIANS 3:18

Paul was writing to Greeks, and Greeks admired wisdom above all else. If Paul were writing to Americans today, he might say, "If you consider yourself successful, you're going to have to fail in the world's eyes in order to succeed in God's eyes."

1 Corinthians 3:18–23
Psalm 24
Luke 5:1–11

*I am not conscious of anything against me, but I do not thereby stand
acquitted; the one who judges me is the Lord.*

—1 CORINTHIANS 4:4

Conscience is unreliable. We often feel just fine about
behavior that should bring us to our knees in repentance.
"Conscience must be informed and moral judgment
enlightened. A well-formed conscience is upright and
truthful. It formulates its judgments according to reason, in
conformity with the true good willed by the wisdom of the
Creator" (*Catechism of the Catholic Church*, 1783).

1 Corinthians 4:1–5
Psalm 37
Luke 5:33–39

To this very hour we go hungry and thirsty, we are poorly clad and roughly treated, we wander about homeless and we toil, working with our own hands. When ridiculed, we bless; when persecuted, we endure; when slandered, we respond gently. We have become like the world's rubbish, the scum of all, to this very moment.

—1 CORINTHIANS 4:11–13

If you follow a man whose idea of leadership is to wash feet and whose idea of conquering is to die on a cross, you might end up with a life like St. Paul's.

1 Corinthians 4:6b–15
Psalm 145
Luke 6:1–5

For where two or three are gathered together in my name, there am I in the midst of them.

—MATTHEW 18:20

On the one hand, Jesus' words indicate that we don't have to be in a cathedral full of people in order to attract Jesus' attention. On the other hand, they indicate that Jesus comes to us in community, even if the community is as small as two or three people.

Ezekiel 33:7–9
Psalm 95
Romans 13:8–10
Matthew 18:15–20

We know that all things work for good for those who love God, who are called according to his purpose.

—ROMANS 8:28

God can use terrible things to bring good into the world. Mary's heart was broken when her son was crucified, but Jesus' resurrection brings hope to the whole human race.

Micah 5:1–4a or Romans 8:28–30
Psalm 13
Matthew 1:1–16, 18–23 or 1:18–23

Now indeed [then] it is, in any case, a failure on your part that you have lawsuits against one another. Why not rather put up with injustice? Why not rather let yourselves be cheated?

—1 CORINTHIANS 6:7

Sometimes justice is just too costly. Sometimes it's better to let go of our grudges and get on with life.

1 Corinthians 6:1–11
Psalm 149
Luke 6:12–19

*If you marry, however, you do not sin, nor does an unmarried woman
sin if she marries; but such people will experience affliction in their
earthly life, and I would like to spare you that.*

—1 CORINTHIANS 7:28

It's a good thing St. Paul didn't have a wife and kids—he
lived dangerously, and he rarely stayed in the same place
for more than a few months. Celibacy made sense for
people who expected Christ's return at any moment and
were called to work 24/7 in the meantime. But the apostles
did not make celibacy a rule. Most, including St. Peter,
were married (1 Corinthians 9:5).

1 Corinthians 7:25–31
Psalm 45
Luke 6:20–26

{K}nowledge inflates with pride, but love builds up.

—1 CORINTHIANS 8:1

Ideally knowledge and love work together. If they can't,
love trumps knowledge every time.

1 Corinthians 8:1b–7, 11–13
Psalm 139
Luke 6:27–38

Every athlete exercises discipline in every way. They do it to win a perishable crown, but we an imperishable one.

—1 CORINTHIANS 9:25

Last month the world watched in awe as young athletes, fortified by years of arduous training, competed for Olympic glory. What disciplines help keep you fit as a follower of Jesus Christ?

1 Corinthians 9:16–19, 22b–27
Psalm 84
Luke 6:39–42

You cannot drink the cup of the Lord and also the cup of demons. You cannot partake of the table of the Lord and of the table of demons.

—1 CORINTHIANS 10:21

There are no part-time Christians.

1 Corinthians 10:14–22
Psalm 116
Luke 6:43–49

Who, though he was in the form of God,
did not regard equality with God something to be grasped.
—PHILIPPIANS 2:6

Instead of building himself up, Jesus emptied himself.
Instead of aiming for a CEO's corner office, he became a
skilled laborer. Instead of doing things his way, he obeyed
his Father. Instead of living a fulfilling life, he died in
shame. "Because of this, God greatly exalted him" (2:9).

Numbers 21:4b–9
Psalm 78
Philippians 2:6–11
John 3:13–17

I hear the whispers of the crowd;
terrors are all around me.
They conspire against me;
they plot to take my life.
But I trust in you, LORD;
I say, "You are my God."
—PSALM 31:14–15

What does it mean to trust in God? Does it mean he will always rescue us from danger? But all of us will eventually die, and some, like Jesus, will die violently. Will we continue to trust God when death is staring us in the face?

1 Corinthians 11:17–26, 33
Psalm 31
John 19:25–27 or Luke 2:33–35

Now the body is not a single part, but many. . . .

Now you are Christ's body, and individually parts of it.
—1 CORINTHIANS 12:14, 27

Some people want their parish to be a place where people
who think alike, dress alike, vote alike, and play alike
gather to worship God in comfort and harmony. But
that's not what the Body of Christ looks like. In a healthy
body, many different parts work together. Feet are poor
substitutes for ears, and the liver can't do the work of the
esophagus—which is why all are needed.

1 Corinthians 12:12–14, 27–31a
Psalm 100
Luke 7:11–17

{I}f I have the gift of prophecy and comprehend all mysteries and all knowledge; if I have all faith so as to move mountains, but do not have love, I am nothing. If I give away everything I own, and if I hand my body over so that I may boast but do not have love, I gain nothing.

—1 CORINTHIANS 13:2–3

Without love, what would a church made up of prophets, mystics, scholars, miracle workers, philanthropists, and martyrs be like? Would you want to be a part of it?

1 Corinthians 12:31–13:13
Psalm 33
Luke 7:31–35

For I handed on to you as of first importance what I also received:
that Christ died for our sins in accordance with the scriptures; that he
was buried; that he was raised on the third day in accordance with the
scriptures; that he appeared to Cephas, then to the Twelve.

—1 CORINTHIANS 15:3–5

This is the gospel, the Good News: Christ died, was
buried, and rose again. His resurrection was real, not
imaginary or metaphorical; many people witnessed the
risen Christ. Because of his death, we can have eternal life.
The gospel gives us reason to hope.

1 Corinthians 15:1–11
Psalm 118
Luke 7:36–50

{I}f Christ has not been raised, your faith is vain; you are still in your sins. Then those who have fallen asleep in Christ have perished. If for this life only we have hoped in Christ, we are the most pitiable people of all.

—1 CORINTHIANS 15:17–19

But Christ *has* been raised. Our faith is fruitful. Our sins have been forgiven. We will see our loved ones again. Our hope in Christ is for this life and the next, and we are the most joyous people of all!

1 Corinthians 15:12–20
Psalm 17
Luke 8:1–3

• ST. ANDREW KIM TAEGON, PRIEST AND MARTYR, AND ST. PAUL CHONG
HASANG, MARTYR, AND THEIR COMPANIONS, MARTYRS •

But someone may say, "How are the dead raised? With what kind of body will they come back?" . . .

It is sown corruptible; it is raised incorruptible. It is sown dishonorable; it is raised glorious. It is sown weak; it is raised powerful. It is sown a natural body; it is raised a spiritual body.

—1 CORINTHIANS 15:35, 42–44

Forget about angels strumming miniature harps on wispy clouds. Our resurrection life will be more, not less, than our earthly life. This world is a faint shadow; the world to come is solid, bright reality.

1 Corinthians 15:35–37, 42–49
Psalm 56
Luke 8:4–15

When those who had started about five o'clock came, each received the usual daily wage. So when the first came, they thought that they would receive more, but each of them also got the usual wage.

—MATTHEW 20:9–10

What would you think of that boss if you had worked hard all day? What would you think if you had started just before closing time? What does the boss's strange behavior say about the kingdom of heaven?

Isaiah 55:6–9
Psalm 145
Philippians 1:20c–24, 27a
Matthew 20:1–16a

Refuse no one the good on which he has a claim
when it is in your power to do it for him.
Say not to your neighbor, "Go, and come again,
tomorrow I will give," when you can give at once.

—PROVERBS 3:27–28

Are you generous (as opposed to stingy)? Or are you
prudent (as opposed to reckless)? Whatever your style of
financial management, do you readily give a portion of
your income to help the needy?

Proverbs 3:27–34
Psalm 15
Luke 8:16–18

All the ways of a man may be right in his own eyes,
but it is the LORD who proves hearts.

—PROVERBS 21:2

Or perhaps all my ways are wrong in my own eyes—it is
still the Lord who judges. And the Lord is gracious.

Proverbs 21:1–6, 10–13
Psalm 119
Luke 8:19–21

SEPTEMBER 24

{G}ive me neither poverty nor riches;
[provide me only with the food I need;]
Lest, being full, I deny you,
saying, "Who is the LORD?"
Or, being in want, I steal,
and profane the name of my God.
—PROVERBS 30:8–9

There is a thin line separating "enough" from "too much."
Why do I never think I have enough, no matter how much
I acquire?

Proverbs 30:5–9
Psalm 119
Luke 9:1–6

⊰ 300 ⊱

SEPTEMBER 25

What profit has man from all the labor
which he toils at under the sun?
One generation passes and another comes,
but the world forever stays.
—ECCLESIASTES 1:3–4

However much wealth we accumulate, we can't take it with us. Here's a wise comment from Ecclesiastes 5:17: "{I}t is well for a man to eat and drink and enjoy all the fruits of his labor under the sun during the limited days of the life which God gives him; for this is his lot."

Ecclesiastes 1:2–11
Psalm 90
Luke 9:7–9

There is an appointed time for everything,
and a time for every affair under the heavens.
A time to be born, and a time to die;
a time to plant, and a time to uproot the plant.

—ECCLESIASTES 3:1–2

When seemingly healthy people die suddenly, we may say they died too soon, even if they were in their nineties. When people suffer for years before finally dying, we may say they died too late, even if they were in their forties. How hard it can be to have the psalmist's faith: "I trust in you, LORD; / I say, 'You are my God.' / My times are in your hands" (Psalm 31:15–16).

Ecclesiastes 3:1–11
Psalm 144
Luke 9:18–22

SEPTEMBER 27

Remember your Creator in the days of your youth,
before the evil days come
And the years approach of which you will say,
I have no pleasure in them.

—ECCLESIASTES 12:1

Don't always put work before play. Don't wait until you retire to pursue your dreams. Don't promise yourself that later you'll say, "I love you" to the important people in your life. Don't wait until you're in a nursing home to turn to God. The time God has given you is now.

Ecclesiastes 11:9–12:8
Psalm 90
Luke 9:43b–45

A man had two sons. He came to the first and said, "Son, go out and work in the vineyard today." He said in reply, "I will not," but afterwards he changed his mind and went. The man came to the other son and gave the same order. He said in reply, "Yes, sir," but did not go. Which of the two did his father's will?

—MATTHEW 21:28–31

That depends. Once the grumpy one got to the vineyard, did he do his work well? And why didn't the agreeable one go? What did he do instead? In any case, poor old Dad. How happy he'd be if one day both sons said, "Yes, sir" and headed straight for the vineyard.

Ezekiel 18:25–28
Psalm 25
Philippians 2:1–11 or 2:1–5
Matthew 21:28–32

Amen, amen, I say to you, you will see the sky opened and the angels of God ascending and descending on the Son of Man.

—JOHN 1:51

Jacob dreamed about angels going up and down a stairway between earth and heaven (Genesis 28:10–15). When he woke up, he said, "Truly, the LORD is in this spot, although I did not know it!" (28:16). In today's Gospel, Jesus is telling Nathanael that someday he, like Jacob, will know that God is with him. Someday he will understand that the Son of man is the stairway connecting earth and heaven.

Daniel 7:9–10, 13–14 or Revelation 12:7–12a
Psalm 138
John 1:47–51

Why is light given to the toilers,
and life to the bitter in spirit?

—JOB 3:20

This is part of Job's anguished cry at the beginning of the
book that bears his name. He has lost everything—his
wealth, his children, his health. Why is God treating him
this way? Why must a good person suffer? The book of
Job is a powerful poem about God and human suffering.
If Job's questions are also yours, read the entire book.
But watch out for Job's friends—they give him tons of
wrongheaded advice.

Job 3:1–3, 11–17, 20–23
Psalm 88
Luke 9:51–56

{H}ow can a man be justified before God? . . .
God is wise in heart and mighty in strength. . . .
He removes the mountains before they know it.

—JOB 9:2, 4–5

"I have always wanted to become a saint. Unfortunately when I have compared myself with the saints, I have always found that there is the same difference between the saints and me as there is between a mountain whose summit is lost in the clouds and a humble grain of sand trodden underfoot by passers-by. Instead of being discouraged, I told myself: God would not make me wish for something impossible and so, in spite of my littleness, I can aim at being a saint" (St. Thérèse).

Job 9:1–12, 14–16
Psalm 88
Luke 9:57–62

I know that my Vindicator lives,
and that he will at last stand forth upon the dust;
Whom I myself shall see:
my own eyes, not another's, shall behold him,
And from my flesh I shall see God.
—JOB 19:25, 27, 26

Job has lost everything, his wife despises him, and his
friends tell him that all his misfortunes are his own fault.
And yet Job believes that before he dies, God will declare
him innocent. Faith is easy when things are going our way.
Faith like Job's is mind-boggling.

Job 19:21–27
Psalm 91
Matthew 18:1–5, 10

Then the LORD *addressed Job out of the storm and said: . . .*

Tell me, if you know all:
Which is the way to the dwelling place of light,
and where is the abode of darkness,
That you may take them to their boundaries
and set them on their homeward paths?

—JOB 38:1, 18–20

In a wild and magnificent poem, God reveals himself as the One who created and maintains the universe, whose wisdom and power are beyond human understanding. Read chapters 38 to 41 aloud, and be overwhelmed by God's power and beauty. God does not directly answer Job's questions, but after seeing God, Job has nothing more to say.

Job 38:1, 12–21; 40:3–5
Psalm 139
Luke 10:13–16

OCTOBER 4

Then Job answered the LORD and said:

I know that you can do all things,
and that no purpose of yours can be hindered. . . .
I had heard of you by word of mouth,
but now my eye has seen you.
Therefore I disown what I have said,
and repent in dust and ashes.

—JOB 42:1–2, 5–6

In a world full of pain, sorrow, and death, can God be trusted? Job thinks so, because he has seen God's glory.

Job 42:1–3, 5–6, 12–17
Psalm 119
Luke 10:17–24

Therefore, I say to you, the kingdom of God will be taken away from you and given to a people that will produce its fruit.

—MATTHEW 21:43

What is the "fruit" of the kingdom? Perhaps the Sermon on the Mount (Matthew 5–7) summarizes it best. It is goodness that comes from the heart, a desire to serve rather than to gain status, and trust in God's provision.

Isaiah 5:1–7
Psalm 80
Philippians 4:6–9
Matthew 21:33–43

{T}here are some who are disturbing you and wish to pervert the gospel of Christ. But even if we or an angel from heaven should preach [to you] a gospel other than the one that we preached to you, let that one be accursed!

—GALATIANS 1:7–8

Paul is writing to people who don't really know what they believe. They have become Christians, but they don't understand the heart of the gospel. They aren't sure how Christianity is different from other religions. The letter to the Galatians is passionate because Paul loves these people and fears for their souls.

Galatians 1:6–12
Psalm 111
Luke 10:25–37

[God], who from my mother's womb had set me apart and called me through his grace, was pleased to reveal his Son to me, so that I might proclaim him to the Gentiles.

—GALATIANS 1:15–16

Nothing but a direct call from God could have persuaded Paul—formerly Saul, persecutor of Christians—to proclaim Christ to the Gentiles. This was such an about-face in his life that it still amazed him to think of it. But he was even more amazed that the Galatians, who also had been "called . . . by [the] grace [of Christ]," could be considering "a different gospel," a perversion of the Good News (1:6).

Galatians 1:13–24
Psalm 139
Luke 10:38–42

And when Cephas came to Antioch, I opposed him to his face because he clearly was wrong.

—GALATIANS 2:11

Ever get tired of "church wars"—disagreements about theology, policy, liturgy, music, and petty things that can make parish life challenging? We're in good company: even St. Peter (aka Cephas) and St. Paul had a hard time getting along. And, you know, it wasn't necessarily a bad thing. Their disagreements forced the early church to clarify its teachings and follow Christ more closely.

Galatians 2:1–2, 7–14
Psalm 117
Luke 11:1–4

*O stupid Galatians! Who has bewitched you . . . ? I want to learn
only this from you: did you receive the Spirit from works of the law, or
from faith in what you heard?*

—GALATIANS 3:1–2

The Galatians had begun to think that faith in Christ was
not enough. Once pagans, now Christians, they were on
the road to becoming Jews as well. Stop! said Paul. Faith
in Christ is everything. You received the Spirit when you
came to faith. Abraham himself was blessed because of his
faith (3:7–9). Don't even consider giving up faith in Christ
for something less!

Galatians 3:1–5
Luke 1:69–70, 71–72, 73–75
Luke 11:5–13

For all who depend on works of the law are under a curse; for it is written, "Cursed be everyone who does not persevere in doing all the things written in the book of the law."

—GALATIANS 3:10

Isn't following the law good? Well, yes. Paul had high regard for the law. But the problem shows up in the word *depend.* Can we depend on our keeping the law to make us the kind of people we want to be? No, because we will continually get tripped up by our own weaknesses. The law can show where we go wrong, but it can't help us go right. Only Jesus can give us the strength to do right, and only Jesus can forgive us when we fail.

Galatians 3:7–14
Psalm 111
Luke 11:15–26

For all of you who were baptized into Christ have clothed yourselves with Christ. There is neither Jew nor Greek, there is neither slave nor free person, there is not male and female; for you are all one in Christ Jesus.

—GALATIANS 3:27–28

And every day may God help us put away our divisions and grow into our oneness in Christ!

Galatians 3:22–29
Psalm 105
Luke 11:27–28

OCTOBER 12

The kingdom of heaven may be likened to a king who gave a wedding feast for his son.

—MATTHEW 22:2

Instead of accepting the invitation graciously, the people invited to the wedding feast refused it, ignored it, and even mistreated and killed the king's servants for delivering it. Of the mixed lot who ended up coming to the feast, one behaved so badly that the king had to call in the royal bouncers.

You'd think people would prize their invitations to a royal wedding. But only a few of the many who are invited do.

Isaiah 25:6–10a
Psalm 23
Philippians 4:12–14, 19–20
Matthew 22:1–14 or 22:1–10

For freedom Christ set us free; so stand firm and do not submit again to the yoke of slavery.

—GALATIANS 5:1

Christ has set us free from the law's condemnation, the devil's accusations, and our own sinful natures. We are like liberated slaves, acquitted defendants, cured patients. Why ever would we want to go back to the mess we were in?

Galatians 4:22–24, 26–27, 31–5:1
Psalm 113
Luke 11:29–32

For in Christ Jesus, neither circumcision nor uncircumcision counts for anything, but only faith working through love.
—GALATIANS 5:6

The Galatian converts were arguing over priorities. Was circumcision necessary? Did Christians have to keep Jewish law? Paul, a Jewish law keeper himself, said no. Keeping the law was fine—as long as the keeper did not make the law more important than love.

Galatians 5:1–6
Psalm 119
Luke 11:37–41

{T}he fruit of the Spirit is love, joy, peace, patience, kindness, generosity, faithfulness, gentleness, self-control. Against such there is no law.

—GALATIANS 5:22–23

When a person's life shows the fruit of the Spirit, the law becomes superfluous. What could the law do that the Spirit has not already done?

Galatians 5:18–25
Psalm 1
Luke 11:42–46

Blessed be the God and Father of our Lord Jesus Christ, who has blessed us in Christ with every spiritual blessing in the heavens, as he chose us in him, before the foundation of the world, to be holy and without blemish before him.

—EPHESIANS 1:3–4

The letter to the Ephesians challenges our individualistic way of thinking. The letter is about the church—not as a group of individuals, but as the community of God's people in Christ. Christ chose the church and blessed it. Christ makes the church holy. As part of the community, we too have been chosen, blessed, and made holy.

Ephesians 1:1–10
Psalm 98
Luke 11:47–54

*In him you also, who have heard the word of truth, the gospel
of your salvation, and have believed in him, were sealed with the
promised holy Spirit.*

—EPHESIANS 1:13

The church began nearly two thousand years ago when
the apostles and other believers received the Holy Spirit at
Pentecost. It continues with all who hear and believe. You
and I have been chosen and sealed with the Holy Spirit,
just as the apostles were.

Ephesians 1:11–14
Psalm 33
Luke 12:1–7

Luke is the only one with me.

—2 TIMOTHY 4:11

St. Luke wasn't one of the Twelve; in fact, he was a Gentile. St. Paul, with whom he often traveled, called him the "beloved physician" (Colossians 4:14). He is traditionally considered the author of two scriptural books, Luke and Acts. According to an ancient tradition, Luke painted icons of Mary, and his Gospel is the source for most of what we know about her. He was faithful to Christ and to St. Paul, and his influence on the church continues to this day.

2 Timothy 4:10–17b
Psalm 145
Luke 10:1–9

OCTOBER 19

*He said to them, "Whose image is this and whose inscription?" They
replied, "Caesar's." At that he said to them, "Then repay to Caesar
what belongs to Caesar and to God what belongs to God."*

—MATTHEW 22:20–21

The early Christians paid taxes, but they refused to burn
incense to the emperor or say "Caesar is Lord"—and some
were executed because of their refusal. Where do we draw
the line between what belongs to Caesar and what belongs
to God?

Isaiah 45:1, 4–6
Psalm 96
1 Thessalonians 1:1–5b
Matthew 22:15–21

But God, who is rich in mercy, because of the great love he had for us,
even when we were dead in our transgressions, brought us to life with
Christ (by grace you have been saved), raised us up with him, and
seated us with him in the heavens in Christ Jesus, that in the ages to
come he might show the immeasurable riches of his grace in his kindness
to us in Christ Jesus.

—EPHESIANS 2:4–7

How is it that the church exists after two thousand
troubled years? It is not because we are good, but because
God is merciful.

Ephesians 2:1–10
Psalm 100
Luke 12:13–21

*He came and preached peace to you who were far off and peace
to those who were near, for through him we both have access
in one Spirit to the Father.*

—EPHESIANS 2:17–18

In the church, old divisions—"the dividing wall of enmity"
(2:14)—are supposed to break down. How can factions
exist where people submit to one another, forgive one
another, look out for one another's well-being, and practice
humility?

Ephesians 2:12–22
Psalm 85
Luke 12:35–38

OCTOBER 22

When you read this you can understand my insight into the mystery of Christ, . . . that the Gentiles are coheirs, members of the same body, and copartners in the promise in Christ Jesus through the gospel.

—EPHESIANS 3:4, 6

In the church, *everyone* is welcome as part of Christ's Body. Long-standing feuds make no difference, because Christ has forgiven the sins of both sides, and because we Christians love our enemies . . . don't we?

Ephesians 3:2–12
Isaiah 12:2–3, 4bcd, 5–6
Luke 12:39–48

Now to him who is able to accomplish far more than all we ask or imagine, by the power at work within us, to him be glory in the church and in Christ Jesus to all generations, forever and ever. Amen.

—EPHESIANS 3:20–21

What are your dreams for your parish? For the church around the world? Do they seem far-fetched or even impossible? There is "power at work within us"—within the church—"to accomplish far more than all we ask or imagine."

Ephesians 3:14–21
Psalm 33
Luke 12:49–53

*I . . . urge you to live in a manner worthy of the call you have received,
with all humility and gentleness, with patience, bearing with one
another through love, striving to preserve the unity of the spirit through
the bond of peace.*

—EPHESIANS 4:1–3

Read that description again. Is that how we live? All the
time? That's how we have to live if we really want the
church to embrace all kinds of people, even people who
are quite different from us.

Ephesians 4:1–6
Psalm 24
Luke 12:54–59

*{G}race was given to each of us according to the measure
of Christ's gift. . . .*

*{H}e gave some as apostles, others as prophets, others as evangelists,
others as pastors and teachers, to equip the holy ones for the work of
ministry, for building up the body of Christ.*

—EPHESIANS 4:7, 11–12

Notice who is supposed to be doing the work of ministry.
Not just apostles, prophets, evangelists, pastors, and
teachers, but the "holy ones"—in other words, everybody
in the church. Those we usually think of as ministers are
actually meant to be coaches for the rest of us, equipping
us to minister.

Ephesians 4:7–16
Psalm 122
Luke 13:1–9

OCTOBER 26

You shall love the Lord, your God, with all your heart, with all your soul, and with all your mind. This is the greatest and the first commandment. The second is like it: You shall love your neighbor as yourself.

—MATTHEW 22:37–39

We've been reading in Galatians and Ephesians about how the Holy Spirit makes a complicated legal system unnecessary and allows people of all backgrounds to come together in harmony. Jesus' summary of the law says the same thing in just a few words: Love God, love your neighbor. We can learn Jesus' words in just a few seconds, but it takes a lifetime to put them into practice.

Exodus 22:20–26
Psalm 18
1 Thessalonians 1:5c–10
Matthew 22:34–40

Be sure of this, that no immoral or impure or greedy person . . . has any inheritance in the kingdom of Christ and of God.

Let no one deceive you with empty arguments, for because of these things the wrath of God is coming upon the disobedient.

—EPHESIANS 5:5–6

Whom do we most admire? People with power, even if they got it immorally? Sexy people? Rich people, especially if they're also powerful and sexy? Oh yes, and Mother Teresa—but would we want to live as she did?

Ephesians 4:32–5:8
Psalm 1
Luke 13:10–17

*When day came, he called his disciples to himself, and from them he
chose Twelve, whom he also named apostles.*

—LUKE 6:13

Quick—write down the names of the twelve apostles, or
as many as you can remember. I'm guessing that today's
honored saints didn't make your list unless you noticed
their names at the top of this page. Little is known about
Simon the Zealot and Judas "son of James" (Luke 6:16;
aka St. Jude, patron of lost causes). Neither was as famous
as the other Simon, Simon Peter, or as infamous as the
other Judas, Judas Iscariot. But in the kingdom of heaven,
faithfulness is more important than fame.

Ephesians 2:19–22
Psalm 19
Luke 6:12–16

Children, obey your parents. . . . Fathers, do not provoke your children to anger. . . .

Slaves, be obedient to your human masters. . . . Masters, . . . stop bullying.

—EPHESIANS 6:1, 4–5, 9

In this final week before the national election, we know full well that unity is hard to achieve. Even in the church, it's hard to keep the peace. St. Paul's practical advice for creating and maintaining unity is based on one principle: "Be subordinate to one another out of reverence for Christ" (5:21). Imagine what the church would be like if every member willingly put others' needs ahead of his or her own.

Ephesians 6:1–9
Psalm 145
Luke 13:22–30

Put on the armor of God so that you may be able to stand firm against the tactics of the devil. For our struggle is not with flesh and blood but with the principalities, with the powers, with the world rulers of this present darkness, with the evil spirits in the heavens.

—EPHESIANS 6:11–12

"And though this world, with devils filled,
should threaten to undo us,
we will not fear, for God has willed
his truth to triumph through us."
("A Mighty Fortress Is Our God")

Ephesians 6:10–20
Psalm 144
Luke 13:31–35

I am confident of this, that the one who began a good work in you will continue to complete it until the day of Christ Jesus.

—PHILIPPIANS 1:6

What God starts, God finishes.

Philippians 1:1–11
Psalm 111
Luke 14:1–6

After this I had a vision of a great multitude, which no one could count, from every nation, race, people, and tongue. They stood before the throne and before the Lamb, wearing white robes and holding palm branches in their hands.

—REVELATION 7:9

See the brass bands and the parades. Hear the trumpets wail. Rejoice at being part of the great multitude standing before the heavenly throne! "Oh, Lord, I want to be in that number, / When the saints go marching in."

Revelation 7:2–4, 9–14
Psalm 24
1 John 3:1–3
Matthew 5:1–12a

And this is the will of the one who sent me, that I should not lose
anything of what he gave me, but that I should raise it [on] the last day.
For this is the will of my Father, that everyone who sees the Son and
believes in him may have eternal life, and I shall raise him
[on] the last day.

—JOHN 6:39–40

"'Death is swallowed up in victory.
Where, O death, is your victory?
Where, O death, is your sting?' . . .

"{T}hanks be to God who gives us the victory through our
Lord Jesus Christ" (1 Corinthians 15:54–55, 57).

Wisdom 3:1–9
Psalm 27
Romans 5:5–11 or 6:3–9
John 6:37–40

Do nothing out of selfishness or out of vainglory; rather, humbly regard others as more important than yourselves, each looking out not for his own interests, but [also] everyone for those of others.

—PHILIPPIANS 2:3–4

Tomorrow the exhausting American political campaign finally concludes. Do you know of any candidates who seem to be living by St. Paul's advice to the Philippians? They are probably the only ones who can safely handle power.

Philippians 2:1–4
Psalm 131
Luke 14:12–14

{H}e emptied himself,
taking the form of a slave,
coming in human likeness;
and found human in appearance,
he humbled himself,
becoming obedient to death,
even death on a cross.

—PHILIPPIANS 2:7–8

The gospel turns words like *winning* and *victory* inside out.
Jesus' power is based not on a landslide or even a narrow
margin but on self-sacrifice.

Philippians 2:5–11
Psalm 22
Luke 14:15–24

So then, my beloved, . . . work out your salvation with fear and trembling. For God is the one who, for his good purpose, works in you both to desire and to work.

—PHILIPPIANS 2:12–13

All our desires for goodness and beauty and truth come from God. All our actions to make the world a better place are achieved through God's power. In God's presence we may tremble because we know we are not "clean of heart" (Matthew 5:8), but we can also take courage because we know God is at work in us.

Philippians 2:12–18
Psalm 27
Luke 14:25–33

{W}hatever gains I had, these I have come to consider a loss because of Christ. More than that, I even consider everything as a loss because of the supreme good of knowing Christ Jesus my Lord.

—PHILIPPIANS 3:7–8

St. Paul could have become a world-renowned rabbi and scholar. St. Francis of Assisi could have taken over the business of his father, a wealthy cloth merchant. Blessed Mother Teresa of Calcutta could have continued working as a high school principal. But all of them thought that answering Jesus' call was more important than worldly success.

Philippians 3:3–8a
Psalm 105
Luke 15:1–10

Join with others in being imitators of me.
—PHILIPPIANS 3:17

For most of us, the better motto is "Do as I say, not as I do." And yet people do imitate us, for good or for ill. Our children. Our friends. Our coworkers. People we don't even know. Is that comforting or alarming?

Philippians 3:17–4:1
Psalm 122
Luke 16:1–8

*I have learned, in whatever situation I find myself, to be self-sufficient.
I know indeed how to live in humble circumstances; I know also how to
live with abundance. . . . I have learned the secret of being well fed and
of going hungry, of living in abundance and of being in need.*

—PHILIPPIANS 4:11–12

Paul did not have a fancy lifestyle to maintain—or credit
cards with which to maintain it. He could be self-sufficient
because he was adaptable.

Philippians 4:10–19
Psalm 112
Luke 16:9–15

He made a whip out of cords and drove them all out of the temple area, with the sheep and oxen, and spilled the coins of the money-changers and overturned their tables, and to those who sold doves he said, "Take these out of here, and stop making my Father's house a marketplace."

—JOHN 2:15–16

What made Jesus angry? The noise and confusion that kept people from hearing the prayers? The bargaining and trickery as merchants and purchasers made deals? The implication that God's grace could be bought and sold, when in reality it is free and abundant? Do we still turn the church into a marketplace today?

Ezekiel 47:1–2, 8–9, 12
Psalm 84
1 Corinthians 3:9c–11, 16–17
John 2:13–22

For a bishop as God's steward must be blameless, not arrogant, not irritable, not a drunkard, not aggressive, not greedy for sordid gain, but hospitable, a lover of goodness, temperate, just, holy, and self-controlled.

—TITUS 1:7–8

"For how shall he instruct others to rule that passion, who has not taught himself? For power leads on to many temptations, it makes a man more harsh and difficult to please, even him that was very mild, surrounding him with so many occasions of anger. If he have not previously practiced himself in this virtue, he will grow harsh, and will injure and destroy much that is under his rule" (St. John Chrysostom).

Titus 1:1–9
Psalm 24
Luke 17:1–6

{O}lder women should be reverent in their behavior, not slanderers, not addicted to drink, teaching what is good, so that they may train younger women to love their husbands and children.

—TITUS 2:3–4

The twentieth-century psychologist Erik Erikson wrote of eight life stages, each with its own developmental task. In order to avoid self-absorption and stagnation, mature adults must choose *generativity*. Fostering growth in younger people is an excellent way to be generative.

Titus 2:1–8, 11–14
Psalm 37
Luke 17:7–10

But when the kindness and generous love
of God our savior appeared,
not because of any righteous deeds we had done
but because of his mercy,
he saved us through the bath of rebirth
and renewal by the holy Spirit,
whom he richly poured out on us
through Jesus Christ our savior,
so that we might be justified by his grace
and become heirs in hope of eternal life.

—TITUS 3:4–7

If Scripture is completely clear about one thing, it's this: only God can fix our broken world. And that is exactly what God is doing.

Titus 3:1–7
Psalm 23
Luke 17:11–19

Perhaps this is why he was away from you for a while, that you might have him back forever, no longer as a slave but more than a slave, a brother.

—PHILEMON 15–16

A slave, Onesimus, had run away from Philemon, his Christian master. Onesimus met Paul, was converted to Christianity, and was now on his way back to Philemon. Some people have to leave the church for a while in order to meet Christ. When we encounter fugitives from faith, how do we treat them?

Philemon 7–20
Psalm 146
Luke 17:20–25

Anyone who is so "progressive" as not to remain in the teaching of the Christ does not have God; whoever remains in the teaching has the Father and the Son.

—2 JOHN 9

The Gnostics in John's day believed that spirit was much more important than matter. To them, the doctrine of the Incarnation—the Son of God taking on human flesh—was for simple folk. Enlightened people like themselves were too spiritual to think that God could become human. But in Scripture, spirit and matter belong together. Both were involved in the creation of Adam and in the incarnation of Jesus. Both are involved in the new life of every Christian.

2 John 4–9
Psalm 119
Luke 17:26–37

Beloved, you are faithful in all you do for the brothers, especially for strangers; they have testified to your love before the church. Please help them in a way worthy of God to continue their journey. For they have set out for the sake of the Name and are accepting nothing from the pagans. Therefore, we ought to support such persons, so that we may be co-workers in the truth.

—3 JOHN 5–8

When we donate money to Christian missions, we become coworkers with the missionaries.

3 John 5–8
Psalm 112
Luke 18:1–8

NOVEMBER 16

To one he gave five talents; to another, two; to a third, one—to each according to his ability.

—MATTHEW 25:15

Parables make us think, and this one is especially thought provoking. The usual explanation is that we are obliged to use whatever talents we have been given. Some commentators add that in the kingdom of God, risk taking is rewarded. Still others turn the parable inside out. Observing that Jews were forbidden to charge interest, they say that the one-talent man is the hero of the story, because he's the only one with the courage to stand up to the unjust master. He takes a huge risk—and fails. Does fear of "the darkness outside" (25:30) ever keep you from taking necessary risks?

Proverbs 31:10–13, 19–20, 30–31
Psalm 128
1 Thessalonians 5:1–6
Matthew 25:14–30 or 25:14–15, 19–21

I know your works, your labor, and your endurance, and that you cannot tolerate the wicked. . . . Yet I hold this against you: you have lost the love you had at first. Realize how far you have fallen.

—REVELATION 2:2, 4–5

Being a Christian involves more than hard work, grim determination, and good morals. The heart of the Christian faith is love. In St. Paul's classic words, "If I give away everything I own, and if I hand my body over so that I may boast but do not have love, I gain nothing" (1 Corinthians 13:3).

Revelation 1:1–4; 2:1–5
Psalm 1
Luke 18:35–43

NOVEMBER 18

*{Y}ou say, "I am rich and affluent and have no need of anything,"
and yet do not realize that you are wretched, pitiable, poor, blind,
and naked. . . . Those whom I love, I reprove and chastise. Be earnest,
therefore, and repent.*

—REVELATION 3:17, 19

This is God's message to Laodicea, a church that is
"neither cold nor hot" (3:15) but thinks it is pretty cool.
Actually, the church is in total denial. It has no idea that
God is disgusted by its lukewarm state (3:16). The church
needs to repent, but how can it? It doesn't know it's doing
anything wrong.

Revelation 3:1–6, 14–22
Psalm 15
Luke 19:1–10
or (for the memorial of the dedication):
Acts 28:11–16, 30–31
Psalm 98
Matthew 14:22–33

At once I was caught up in spirit. A throne was there in heaven, and on the throne sat one whose appearance sparkled like jasper and carnelian. Around the throne was a halo as brilliant as an emerald. . . . From the throne came flashes of lightning, rumblings, and peals of thunder. Seven flaming torches burned in front of the throne, which are the seven spirits of God.

—REVELATION 4:2–3, 5

Scary books and movies have given the book of Revelation a bad reputation. Yes, it portrays disasters and horrors, but its central message is this: no matter what evil things happen, the universe is being run by a good and powerful God. "Worthy are you, Lord our God, / to receive glory and honor and power" (4:11).

Revelation 4:1–11
Psalm 150
Luke 19:11–28

Worthy are you to receive the scroll
and to break open its seals,
for you were slain and with your blood you purchased for God
those from every tribe and tongue, people and nation.

—REVELATION 5:9

The scroll held information about the future, and only
Jesus was able to open it. What lies ahead for the world?
The nation? My family? Me? Mostly I'd rather not know.
But I do know that Jesus endured more suffering than I'll
ever have to go through, and because of Jesus' resurrection
the future is ultimately safe, no matter what lies between
here and heaven.

Revelation 5:1–10
Psalm 149
Luke 19:41–44

I took the small scroll from the angel's hand and swallowed it. In my mouth it was like sweet honey, but when I had eaten it, my stomach turned sour. Then someone said to me, "You must prophesy again about many peoples, nations, tongues, and kings."

—REVELATION 10:10–11

What is in this mysterious scroll? The sweet foretaste of the coming new earth, when God will "make all things new" (21:5), but also the sour prediction of disaster and suffering for the present world. "Prophesy again," said the voice. Evil will not have the last word. Keep hope alive.

Revelation 10:8–11
Psalm 119
Luke 19:45–48

When {God's witnesses} have finished their testimony, the beast that comes up from the abyss will wage war against them and conquer them and kill them. . . . But after the three and a half days, a breath of life from God entered them. When they stood on their feet, great fear fell on those who saw them.

—REVELATION 11:7, 11

Things are not as they appear. The inhabitants of earth gloat and party because God's witnesses, whose faithfulness has rebuked them, are dead, but God breathes life back into them. Reality will soon break through the earth's protective, deceptive layer, and the glorious God of the universe will be revealed.

Revelation 11:4–12
Psalm 144
Luke 20:27–40

{W}hatever you did for one of these least brothers of mine,
you did for me.

—MATTHEW 25:40

"This Gospel passage, so crucial in understanding Mother Teresa's service to the poor, was the basis of her faith-filled conviction that in touching the broken bodies of the poor she was touching the body of Christ. . . . Mother Teresa highlights the deepest meaning of service—an act of love done to the hungry, thirsty, strangers, naked, sick, prisoners . . . is done to Jesus himself" (Pope John Paul II).

Ezekiel 34:11–12, 15–17
Psalm 23
1 Corinthians 15:20–26, 28
Matthew 25:31–46

• ST. ANDREW DUNG-LAC, PRIEST AND MARTYR, AND HIS COMPANIONS,
MARTYRS •

{T}hese are the ones who follow the Lamb wherever he goes. They have been ransomed as the firstfruits of the human race for God and the Lamb. On their lips no deceit has been found; they are unblemished.

—REVELATION 14:4–5

In the eighteenth and nineteenth centuries, thousands of Christians died for their faith in Vietnam. Most were native laypersons, and most are unknown today. In 1988, Pope John Paul II canonized 117 martyrs of Vietnam. Known or unknown, these faithful saints and martyrs are surely with "the Lamb standing on Mount Zion," singing "a new hymn before the throne" (14:1, 3).

Revelation 14:1–3, 4b–5
Psalm 24
Luke 21:1–4

NOVEMBER 25

• ST. CATHERINE OF ALEXANDRIA, VIRGIN AND MARTYR •

So the angel swung his sickle over the earth and cut the earth's vintage.
He threw it into the great wine press of God's fury.

—REVELATION 14:19

Why is God furious? Check your newspaper. Here are some news items as I write: Forty killed by suicide bomb inside Iraqi military base. Ancient coral reefs destroyed by climate change and disease. Corrupt lobbyist jailed for six years. Church faces hundreds of new abuse claims.

God is furious at whatever destroys his beautiful creation, whatever makes his beloved human beings suffer.

Revelation 14:14–19
Psalm 96
Luke 21:5–11

Great and wonderful are your works,
Lord God almighty.
Just and true are your ways,
O king of the nations. . . .
All the nations will come
and worship before you,
for your righteous acts have been revealed.
—REVELATION 15:3–4

Why, Lord? Why so much suffering? Why me? Why them? Someday we will understand what God has been doing behind the scenes. Someday we will give thanks for the paths we have had to follow. But until then, "we walk by faith, not by sight" (2 Corinthians 5:7).

Revelation 15:1–4
Psalm 98
Luke 21:12–19

Then the angel said to me, "Write this: Blessed are those who have been
called to the wedding feast of the Lamb."

—REVELATION 19:9

And blessed are those who play or squabble or pray with
their families, and those who have more than enough food
to eat and those who rely on the kindness of strangers, and
those who like football and those who would rather take
a brisk walk after dinner, and those who cook food or set
tables or carve the turkey or wash dishes, and those who
receive the Lamb of God in the Eucharistic feast and look
forward to his coming in glory.

Revelation 18:1–2, 21–23; 19:1–3, 9a
Psalm 100
Luke 21:20–28

Then I saw a new heaven and a new earth. The former heaven and the former earth had passed away, and the sea was no more.

—REVELATION 21:1

Scripture is all about second chances. And third chances and fourth chances. Floods destroy the earth, but Noah floats. Israel is enslaved and persecuted, but the Red Sea opens. Jesus is executed and buried, but the tomb bursts open. Evil and destruction rage, but the earth is created all over again.

Revelation 20:1–4, 11–21:2
Psalm 84
Luke 21:29–33

Behold, I am coming soon.
—REVELATION 22:7

Tomorrow a new cycle of the church year begins as we enter the season of Advent, the time of waiting for Christ to come. "The Spirit and the bride say, 'Come.' Let the hearer say, 'Come.' Let the one who thirsts come forward, and the one who wants it receive the gift of life-giving water. . . .

"The one who gives this testimony says, 'Yes, I am coming soon.' Amen! Come, Lord Jesus!" (22:17, 20).

Revelation 22:1–7
Psalm 95
Luke 21:34–36

The liturgical calendar does not count years from January 1 to December 31, but rather from the first Sunday of Advent through the last Saturday of ordinary time. The church year has just ended. Tomorrow begins a new cycle of readings that will continue through November 28, 2009.

If these daily thoughts have blessed you this year, now is the time to get 2009: *A Book of Grace-Filled Days*, by Alice Camille. The readings that follow are taken from that book, so you can switch from 2008 to 2009 anytime this month. Pick it up or order it from your local bookstore, or order it online at www.loyolabooks.org.

NOVEMBER 3 o

Watch, therefore; you do not know when the lord of the house is coming, whether in the evening, or at midnight, or at cockcrow, or in the morning.

—MARK 13:35

Time dribbles through our fingers while we wait. Life falls into a holding pattern in checkout lines, on subway platforms, in airports, or in traffic jams. We await payday, test results, or the first glimpse of the one face that matters. We turn toward what's coming with excitement, dread—and, sometimes, joyful hope. And in Advent, we do one thing more: we wait *watchfully*. God will break into time like a thief. What will the holy one find locked in our hearts?

Isaiah 63:16b–17, 19b; 64:2–7
Psalm 80
1 Corinthians 1:3–9
Mark 13:33–37

Come, let us climb the LORD's mountain,
to the house of the God of Jacob,
That he may instruct us in his ways,
and we may walk in his paths.

—ISAIAH 2:3

After midnight, our small group began the ascent of a mountain on the Sinai Peninsula believed to be the one Moses climbed to meet God. Thirty-three hundred years ago, Moses did it without a guide, a warm coat, or a flashlight. As we climbed, the wind bit hard; I stopped looking over the sheer drop. We made the crest at dawn. Would God be manifest, after our hours of striving? An Arab man sat on top of the mountain, crouched over a fire. "Some tea?" he asked. In English. God was here!

Isaiah 2:1–5
Psalm 122
Matthew 8:5–11

DECEMBER 2

Turning to the disciples in private {Jesus} said, "Blessed are the eyes that see what you see."

—LUKE 10:23

Life is good! From where you are, you can probably see something that would astound prophets and kings of old. Are electric lights gleaming above you? Is food being kept at a carefully calibrated temperature in your fridge? Does a loved one's face smile at you from a photograph? Still, the greatest blessings are seen only through the eyes of faith: the presence of Jesus in word and sacrament, in suffering and healing, in death and fullness of life.

Isaiah 11:1–10
Psalm 72
Luke 10:21–24

DECEMBER 3

• ST. FRANCIS XAVIER, PRIEST •

Even when I walk through a dark valley,
I fear no harm for you are at my side;
your rod and staff give me courage.

—PSALM 23:4

The dark valley haunts us all our lives. Francis Xavier
longed to bring the gospel to China, but after evangelizing
India and Malaysia, he died within sight of his heart's
desire. Our mortality may catch up with us before we pay
off the house, raise the kids, or fulfill our dreams.
The very definition of our humanity may be this: life is
over before we're finished. "Finished" doesn't matter;
it's "faithful" that we're after. Fidelity is the greatest legacy
we can leave behind.

Isaiah 25:6–10a
Psalm 23
Matthew 15:29–37

The LORD is God and has given us light.
—PSALM 118:27

In the eighth century, iconoclasts destroyed sacred images,
believing that the Eucharist alone should represent the
divine on earth. John of Damascus argued that images help
connect us to the invisible realities of heaven. Have you
ever encountered religious art and been captured by the
truth you discovered there? Artists participate in the divine
activity of creation. Surely God still says, through the
artist: "Let there be light."

Isaiah 26:1–6
Psalm 118
Matthew 7:21, 24–27

One thing I ask of the LORD;
this I seek:
To dwell in the LORD's house
all the days of my life,
To gaze on the LORD's beauty,
to visit his temple.

—PSALM 27:4

Looking for God? Look for beauty. Dante understood
this when he wrote *The Divine Comedy* and described the
"Beatific Vision" of God. He borrowed this idea from
the psalmist, but also from Exodus. There, in chapter 33,
Moses begs to see the God he faithfully serves. God gently
refuses—mortal life cannot withstand the sight—but offers
instead to reveal "all my beauty." When we stand in awe of
loveliness, we get a glimpse of what Moses saw.

Isaiah 29:17–24
Psalm 27
Matthew 9:27–31

Cure the sick, raise the dead, cleanse lepers, drive out demons. Without cost you have received; without cost you are to give.

—MATTHEW 10:8

Cure the sick? Who wouldn't unleash such power if they could? I sat with my friend in the oncology unit as he awaited radiation treatment. Surveying a roomful of courageous patients, I fiercely longed for miracles to sweep down and anoint every head. But all I was able to give my friend was a steady gaze into his suffering and hopeful eyes.

Isaiah 30:19–21, 23–26
Psalm 147
Matthew 9:35–10:1, 5a, 6–8

But according to his promise we await new heavens and a new earth in which righteousness dwells.

—2 PETER 3:13

"New" is what we need. The old world is frayed and broken in a lot of places. We mend it from time to time with diplomacy and charity, or prop it up with environmental measures, military threats, and economic incentives. But human history remains the worse for wear. Yet we can't just throw up our hands and abandon the place. It's all we've got! So we continue to work for justice and peace, all the while praying for that kingdom to come.

Isaiah 40:1–5, 9–11
Psalm 85
2 Peter 3:8–14
Mark 1:1–8

Then the angel said to her, "Do not be afraid, Mary, for you have found favor with God."

—LUKE 1:30

Mary's heart was remarkable. Even God fell in love with her! And so have billions of folks since. A Marian sanctuary in Altötting, Bavaria, preserves in silver urns the actual hearts of kings and princes who swore special allegiance to Mary. Probably no one will ever place my heart in a shrine. But there are other ways to surrender our hearts like Mary did.

Genesis 3:9–15, 20
Psalm 98
Ephesians 1:3–6, 11–12
Luke 1:26–38

Tell God's glory among the nations;
among all peoples, God's marvelous deeds.

—PSALM 96:3

Juan Diego was nobody, really. Just a Mexican Indian of a defeated people who had barely survived the bloody European conquest of 1521. Their homes had been burned, their men killed, their women raped, and their temples destroyed. Juan Diego and his people did not have much to live for. Yet to them and in their likeness, the Virgin appeared and promised her protection. Even when you're nobody, heaven is watching.

Isaiah 40:1–11
Psalm 96
Matthew 18:12–14

Come to me, all you who labor and are burdened,
and I will give you rest.

—MATTHEW 11:28

I know a man who was rescued by these simple words.
He was a stockbroker, successful in terms of money,
personal attraction, and career potential. He was also an
alcoholic at the mercy, night and day, of his "gorgeous
thirst." One Advent night, he slumped into the back pew
of a church while Mass was going on. He heard Jesus
promise to take his burden away. How he longed for such
rest! He quit drinking. Today he's proclaiming this hope
to others as a priest.

Isaiah 40:25–31
Psalm 103
Matthew 11:28–30

DECEMBER 11

From the days of John the Baptist until now, the kingdom of heaven suffers violence, and the violent are taking it by force.

—MATTHEW 11:12

Can heaven be taken by force? Or can violence ever serve God's purposes? Scriptures can be gathered to support one side of this argument and the other. Wars have been fought in the name of religion, both armies blessed as they go into battle. Conversions have been gained at the point of a sword. Many simply are frightened into obedience by the pains of hell. Yet how can the realm of a God who is love ever be entered except through love's own free surrender?

Isaiah 41:13–20
Psalm 145
Matthew 11:11–15

Blessed are you who believed that what was spoken to you by the Lord would be fulfilled.

—LUKE 1:45

Visions and angels and saints, oh my! Private revelations are by definition not for everyone, and the church teaches that belief in them is not mandatory. Yet many find the apparitions of Mary both instructive and encouraging to their faith. As the Virgin of Guadalupe, Mary said, "I want to be your mother. I want to right the wrongs." Sure sounds like heaven talking, don't you think?

Zechariah 2:14–17 or Revelation 11:19a; 12:1–6a, 10ab
Psalm 45
Luke 1:26–38 or 1:39–47

How awesome are you, ELIJAH!
Whose glory is equal to yours? . . .
You were taken aloft in a whirlwind,
in a chariot with fiery horses.
—SIRACH 48:4, 9

I always expected God to appear in a glorious display,
as when the fiery chariot snatches Elijah into heaven. I
was hoping for the God of Cecil B. DeMille. Sometimes,
however, God is more like George Burns.

Sirach 48:1–4, 9–11
Psalm 80
Matthew 17:9a, 10–13

When the Jews from Jerusalem sent priests and Levites [to] {John} to ask him, "Who are you?" he admitted and did not deny it, but admitted, "I am not the Messiah."

—JOHN 1:19–20

"Finding yourself" is a highly overrated imperative. It doesn't matter so much that we know precisely who we are—especially since a human being is always growing and changing anyway. But it sure helps to know who we're *not*. We're not God, for one. We're not even close, not on our best days. John's final answer regarding his identity is instructive: he's a voice in an empty place announcing God's arrival. We should all be so clear about our reason for being!

Isaiah 61:1–2a, 10–11
Luke 1:46–50, 53–54
1 Thessalonians 5:16–24
John 1:6–8, 19–28

The utterance of Balaam, son of Beor,
the utterance of the man whose eye is true. . . .
I see him, though not now;
I behold him, though not near:
A star shall advance from Jacob,
and a staff shall rise from Israel.
—NUMBERS 24:15, 17

The whole passage, chapters 22–24, is worth a read. The story of Balaam and his ass is the only anecdote of a talking animal outside of Eden—and the donkey isn't the only ass in the tale. Balaam becomes a true prophet the hard way, by being brought to his knees by God. We all learn humility the hard way, it seems, but it's the only way to become a person "whose eye is true."

Numbers 24:2–7, 15–17a
Psalm 25
Matthew 21:23–27

DECEMBER 16

They shall do no wrong
and speak no lies;
Nor shall there be found in their mouths
a deceitful tongue.
—ZEPHANIAH 3:13

Truth is an attribute of God. It's a big deal in both the Old and the New Testament: giving false testimony earns a "You shall not" among the Ten Commandments. Jesus calls himself "the truth." But we live in an age of spin, image management, retouched photography, and cosmetic surgery. Truth, frankly, is not our deal. Pilate's ancient lament might be raised today: What is truth? How do we become people of truth in an age dependent on illusions?

Zephaniah 3:1–2, 9–13
Psalm 34
Matthew 21:28–32

The scepter shall never depart from Judah.

—GENESIS 49:10

The lineage of Jesus runs through Judah. During the week before Christmas, the church has traditionally honored the human and divine origins of Jesus in the "O Antiphons." We know them as the familiar verses of "O Come, O Come, Emmanuel." The first antiphon, O Wisdom, reminds us that all of creation was ordered by God's own wisdom— the only "intelligent design" we'll ever need. God's wisdom is shared with us as one of the seven gifts of the Holy Spirit. Pray for wisdom. Seek it. Share it.

Genesis 49:2, 8–10
Psalm 72
Matthew 1:1–17

She will bear a son and you are to name him Jesus, because he will save his people from their sins.

—MATTHEW 1:21

Today's antiphon is a Hebrew name: O Adonai. It's a respectful title usually translated "Lord" or "Master." Although God gave the divine name to Moses as "I AM WHO AM," folks were reluctant to abuse the privilege of using it. In John's Gospel, Jesus insists on saying "I AM" a lot—bringing the accusation of blasphemy. St. Paul proclaimed boldly, "Jesus is Lord"—take it or leave it. Most of the time, we leave it. What would happen if we took it seriously?

Jeremiah 23:5–8
Psalm 72
Matthew 1:18–25

An angel of the LORD appeared to the woman and said to her, "Though you are barren and have had no children, yet you will conceive and bear a son."

—JUDGES 13:3

The situation is hopeless, yet God promises the impossible. Is it Mary of Nazareth who receives this news? This time, actually, it's the mother of Samson—but it could just as well have been Sarah, Hannah, the Shunammite woman, or Elizabeth. Or maybe even you or someone you know. God's in the "impossible" business. "O Root of Jesse" is the name we celebrate today, because new life keeps coming from that surprising source.

Judges 13:2–7, 24–25a
Psalm 71
Luke 1:5–25

Therefore the Lord himself will give you this sign: the virgin shall be with child, and bear a son, and shall name him Immanuel.

—ISAIAH 7:14

I'm not always good at reading the signs. The sky may be threatening, but I leave the umbrella behind. My wallet is empty, but I count on finding an ATM wherever I am. I eat past the moment I am full. I'm tempted by easy money, even though I know there's no such thing. O Key of David, unlock my foolish heart and help me take the signs of your truth more seriously!

Isaiah 7:10–14
Psalm 24
Luke 1:26–38

DECEMBER 21

• FOURTH SUNDAY OF ADVENT •

*[. . . according to the revelation of the mystery kept secret for long ages
but now manifested through the prophetic writings . . .]*
—ROMANS 16:25–26

The meaning of the events of our lives often dawns slowly.
What started out as a simple childhood hobby leads to a
lifelong passion. A chance meeting becomes a marriage.
A tiny spiritual tap on the shoulder awakens a religious
vocation. O Radiant Dawn, you arrive on our doorstep
while we are still half-asleep. Open our eyes to the great
blessing you always have in store for us.

2 Samuel 7:1–5, 8b–12, 14a, 16
Psalm 89
Romans 16:25–27
Luke 1:26–38

{The LORD} raises the needy from the dust;
from the ash heap he lifts up the poor,
To seat them with nobles
and make a glorious throne their heritage.

—1 SAMUEL 2:8

In old-world societies, "rich" and "poor" were immutable
social classes. Those born rich tended to remain in such
circles, and those born poor would never amount to much.
Part of the American Dream is the idea that one can arise
from humble beginnings to achieve greatness. Social class
is dismissed as merely an illusion or a temporary condition.
O King of Nations, help us see that the last will be first,
and the first are destined to be last.

1 Samuel 1:24–28
1 Samuel 2:1, 4–8
Luke 1:46–56

DECEMBER 23

• ST. JOHN OF KANTY, PRIEST •

All who heard these things took them to heart, saying, "What, then, will this child be?" For surely the hand of the Lord was with him.

—LUKE 1:66

John, aka the Baptist, seemed destined for greatness. Not much was expected of another John, however—a Polish fellow from Kanty. Ousted from his university professorship under false accusations, he wound up a parish priest in Bohemia. But he didn't protest his treatment: "Fight all error," he said, "but do it with good humor, patience, kindness, and love. Harshness will damage your own soul and spoil the best cause." O Emmanuel, I know well that the harshness I show toward others hurts me most of all.

Malachi 3:1–4, 23–24
Psalm 25
Luke 1:57–66

And you, child, will be called prophet of the Most High,
for you will go before the Lord to prepare his ways,
to give his people knowledge of salvation
through the forgiveness of their sins.

—LUKE 1:76–77

Boil Christianity down to its essence, and you end up with
one word: *forgiveness*. It's no one's favorite word, because
forgiving is one of the toughest things we'll do in this life.
It's an activity that presupposes a grievance, and the last
thing an injured person wants to do is let go of a just cause
for outrage. Eye-for-an-eye justice is the way of the world.
But it's not God's way. Not if Jesus is your Lord.

2 Samuel 7:1–5, 8b–12, 14a, 16
Psalm 89
Luke 1:67–79

DECEMBER 25

And the Word became flesh
and made his dwelling among us,
and we saw his glory,
the glory as of the Father's only Son,
full of grace and truth.

—JOHN 1:14

Love is a word made flesh. There's no point in saying it unless you're going to back it up with substance, with body and blood, sweat and tears. That's how parents show love to their children, lovers to their beloved, friends to their comrades, and soldiers to their country. That's how saints demonstrate their love for the God they follow, all the way to martyrdom. So too the Word of God makes his fragile way into the world, risking all for love's sake.

Vigil:
Isaiah 62:1–5
Psalm 89
Acts 13:16–17, 22–25
Matthew 1:1–25 or 1:18–25

Midnight:
Isaiah 9:1–6
Psalm 96
Titus 2:11–14
Luke 2:1–14

Dawn:
Isaiah 62:11–12
Psalm 97
Titus 3:4–7
Luke 2:15–20

Day:
Isaiah 52:7–10
Psalm 98
Hebrews 1:1–6
John 1:1–18 or 1:1–5, 9–14

The witnesses laid down their cloaks at the feet of a young man named Saul. As they were stoning Stephen, he called out, "Lord Jesus, receive my spirit."

—ACTS 7:58–59

Here is a strange and sudden turning point: the church grieves its first martyr in the hour it introduces its most celebrated missionary. The death of Stephen comes about at the feet of Saul. Saul is hardly an innocent bystander as he collects the coats. He's a ferocious hater of the new religion and its adherents. He regards God's law as immutable and wants to see lawbreakers punished. He must have heard Stephen's confident cries for God's mercy with incredulity.

Acts 6:8–10; 7:54–59
Psalm 31
Matthew 10:17–22

DECEMBER 27

• ST. JOHN, APOSTLE AND EVANGELIST •

What was from the beginning,
what we have heard,
what we have seen with our eyes,
what we looked upon
and touched with our hands
concerns the Word of life.

—1 JOHN 1:1

The evangelists gave their testimony. They stood up in the court of human experience and witnessed to what they themselves had heard, seen, touched, and understood. We continue to benefit from their words, but it isn't enough to memorize and recite what they said. We have to find the courage to testify to what *we* have come to know through our own experiences. What do we really believe?

1 John 1:1–4
Psalm 97
John 20:1a, 2–8

Put on then, as God's chosen ones, holy and beloved, heartfelt compassion, kindness, humility, gentleness, and patience, bearing with one another and forgiving one another, if one has a grievance against another; as the Lord has forgiven you, so must you also do. And over all these put on love, that is, the bond of perfection.

—COLOSSIANS 3:12–14

I can't think of better words with which to advise a family on how to *be* a family. Without humility and gentleness as a foundation, relationships soon collapse under conflict. Without constantly renewed forgiveness (forget the easy math of seventy times seven!), intimacy is impossible. Without love, blood ties devolve into chains. Holy families are, first and foremost, havens of kindness.

Sirach 3:2–7, 12–14 or Genesis 15:1–6; 21:1–3
Psalm 128
Colossians 3:12–21 or 3:12–17 or Hebrews 11:8, 11–12, 17–19
Luke 2:22–40 or 2:22, 39–40

Now, Master, you may let your servant go
in peace, according to your word.
—LUKE 2:29

The old year is on the wane. Time is among God's most
faithful servants, but sooner or later, even time pours itself
out into eternity like a humble tributary into the great
ocean. This past year gave each of us many opportunities
to practice the fruits of the Holy Spirit: love, joy, peace,
patience, kindness, generosity, faithfulness, gentleness,
and self-control. We embraced some, botched others. In
the spirit of reconciliation, let this past year go in peace.
Renew your resolve for the year ahead.

1 John 2:3–11
Psalm 96
Luke 2:22–35

DECEMBER 30

*There was also a prophetess, Anna. . . . She was advanced in years,
having lived seven years with her husband after her marriage, and then
as a widow until she was eighty-four. She never left the temple, but
worshiped night and day with fasting and prayer.*

—LUKE 2:36–37

I know this woman. I think we all do. She gives every spare
moment to the church, every last dime to the needy. She
comes to every meeting and marches in every protest.
Every good cause is her cause. She knows everybody and
remembers the past with wisdom. She's old and her face is
weathered, but she has the high spirits of a teenager and
the optimism of a child. If you catch her praying in a dark
church, she glows.

1 John 2:12–17
Psalm 96
Luke 2:36–40

DECEMBER 31

Children, it is the last hour; and just as you heard that the antichrist was coming, so now many antichrists have appeared. . . . But you have the anointing that comes from the holy one, and you all have knowledge.

—1 JOHN 2:18, 20

Do you believe the end is near? I do. It doesn't take a prophet to know that in every moment, every cell in our bodies is moving toward its expiration date. Antichrists— those who move in a spirit contrary to the will of Christ— are much in evidence. Is our proximity to death and the reality of evil reason to fear? Not if we surrender our lives to the holy one, early and often.

1 John 2:18–21
Psalm 96
John 1:1–18